MIND WARS

The Battle for Your Brain

Ian McFadyen

ALLEN & UNWIN

Allen & Unwin
9 Atchison Street
St Leonards NSW 2065
Australia
Phone: (61 2) 8425 0100
Fax: (61 2) 9906 2218
Email: frontdesk@allen-unwin.com.au
Web: http://www.allenandunwin.com

National Library of Australia
Cataloguing-in-Publication entry:

McFadyen, Ian.
Mind wars: the battle for your brain.

Bibliography.
Includes index.
ISBN 1 86508 316 X

1. Evolution. 2. Human behaviour. I. Title.

576.8

Set in 11/13.5 pt Janson Text by DOCUPRO, Sydney
Printed by Griffin Press Pty Ltd, South Australia

10 9 8 7 6 5 4 3 2 1

CONTENTS

ABOUT THE AUTHOR

Ian McFadyen was born in Melbourne. He attended Melbourne High School where, although his initial love was science, he began to develop an interest in literature and film. He went on to study Arts, Education and Criminology at Melbourne University where he also became involved in theatre and film-making.

Following university he worked as a social worker and a teacher before moving into theatre and television as an actor, director and producer. In the 1980s, he formed his own television production company, producing, among other things, the hugely popular series 'The Comedy Company', which created a boom in Australian television comedy.

Since that time Ian McFadyen has dedicated himself to scriptwriting, teaching young film-makers and writing about entertainment, mass media and the new technologies. He now lives in Brisbane.

INTRODUCTION

FOR CENTURIES HUMAN BEINGS have been perplexed by the self destructiveness of their own species. Wars, feuds, persecution, bigotry, intolerance, brutality, oppression and corruption have dominated every age of human history, leading many people to condemn the human race as inherently evil. Religions have characterised humankind as intrinsically flawed, possessed of original sin and struggling to surpass its evil nature to find a more holy existence. In the 20th century theorists have examined the human race's ancestry, the structure of the brain, the action of hormones, the political system, the monetary system, the class system, child-rearing practices and even diet as an explanation of human behaviour.

This book sets out to show that human behaviour is not a product of instinct nor of any particular social, political or economic system but the result of ongoing battles between self-replicating systems of thought, battles in which human beings are mere pawns but over which they have, mercifully, some control.

This book was originally inspired by Richard Dawkins' 1976 book on genetics *The Selfish Gene*. It was in this work that Dawkins coined the term 'Meme' meaning a behaviour that is spread through a population by imitation. The concept of the Meme promptly verified itself by inspiring a number of enthusiastic books dealing with 'Meme Theory' and 'the new science of the Meme'.

I hasten to point out that *Mind Wars* is *not* a book about Meme Theory. It was not the notion of the Meme that inspired it but rather Dawkins' illuminating clarification that it is not *organisms* that evolve but DNA *molecules*. The idea for this book grew independently out of that concept and, while it deals with the same issues as Meme Theory, it pursues a parallel line of thought.

The focus of this book will be complex *systems of belief* that I will call *doctrines*—which simply means 'something that is taught' (from Latin *docere*, to teach). The building blocks of doctrines—the individual components of belief—will be referred to as *tenets*, another existing English word, which means 'something we hold to be true' (from Latin *tenere*, to hold). From this term I will coin one neologism. The study of tenets and how they control the replication and evolution of doctrines will be called *tenetics*. It is my hope that the study of tenetics will explain how doctrines control human beings.

This book is not an academic work. It is not necessarily a book for people who have read a lot of other books. It does not set out to develop or demolish the works of other theorists. It is based rather on a general knowledge of science, history and human behaviour. Consequently, people more learned than myself may find much to criticise within its pages. Where I have oversimplified complex issues I apologise in advance but it is my intent not to mire the reader in a morass of details or an endless recital of names. At the same time this is not a book of popular psychology, mysticism or conspiracy theory. Tenetics is a serious, scientific attempt to understand the way in which we view the world and ourselves.

But let's start at the beginning.

CHAPTER 1

MULTIPLICATION IS THE NAME OF THE GAME

THE STORY OF EVE

Eve Smith is Communications Manager at Synaptic Systems, a large company with over 2000 employees. Eve wishes to circulate a memo regarding an important meeting to the staff of the company but she has to leave the office in just a few minutes to catch a plane. To complicate matters, her assistant is off sick and the office email system is down. Eve hasn't got time to personally photocopy 2000 copies of the memo and hand them out but she comes up with an ingenious solution. On the top of the memo she writes the following instructions:

MEMO

To: All staff
From: Eve Smith

1. As soon as you receive this memo, photocopy it and give the copy to a colleague who has not seen it yet.
2. Retain this copy and read announcement re meeting below.
3. Announcement re meeting:
   A meeting of all staff is to be held in the auditorium at 9:00 am on Monday, 5 June.

Eve figures that if she hands this memo to one employee before she leaves and if all the employees obey the instructions, the memo will end up being circulated through the whole company. Just before she walks out the door, Eve has second thoughts. She stops and makes a small calculation. Assuming that it takes 15 minutes for an employee to walk to the photocopier, copy the memo and find someone without a copy to pass it to, all the employees will receive a copy of the memo within 500 hours, or about 12 working weeks. This is obviously too long, so Eve modifies the instructions slightly as follows:

MEMO

To: All staff
From: Eve Smith

1. As soon as you receive this memo, photocopy it twice and give the copies to two colleagues who haven't seen it yet.
2. Retain this copy and read announcement re meeting below.
3. Announcement re meeting:
   A meeting of all staff is to be held in the auditorium at 9:00 am on Monday, 5 June.

Assuming that the employees obey the instructions at the top of the memo, the number of memos will multiply every 15 minutes at the rate of 1, 3, 7, 15, 31, 63, 127, 255, 511, 1023, 2047, so that the whole staff will have received the memo after only $2\frac{1}{2}$ hours.

Clearly if the memo specified that every recipient had to make *three* copies and pass them on, the memo would circulate even faster but Eve feels that this is fast enough and does not wish to make too many demands on her colleagues. She prints out one copy of the memo and hands it to a colleague on her way out of the building.

What Eve did in writing her memo was to create a *self-replicating system*. Self-replicating systems are the basis of life on Earth. In the simplest form of self-replication, a single cell divides into two cells that are identical to the original. Those two cells divide into four and then eight and so on. The process of division is activated and controlled by a molecule in the nucleus of the cell called DNA. We can think of the DNA as containing *instructions* for the construction and replication of the cell.

Of course, if the new cells are going to continue to divide they must *also* contain the DNA, so the first thing the DNA must do when it duplicates the cell is to duplicate *itself*. If this did not occur, only one of the new cells would have DNA and it would be the only one that could divide again. The other cell might be able to live and function, but it could not replicate itself.

Like the DNA in a living cell, the instructions to copy Eve's memo *are contained within the memo itself*. The instructions specify the number of copies to be made and distributed. Note that the instructions also include a limit: the employees are only to give a copy to other employees who haven't received one yet. When all employees have received a copy, replication stops.[1]

Biological cells also have mechanisms to limit their replication. If a cell's limitation mechanisms fail, the cell may continue to replicate endlessly, in other words it becomes what we call a cancer cell, which can be dangerous if not fatal to the organism containing it.

Eve's memo could have contained other elements to enhance its chances of replication. It could have contained

---

1   In fact Eve's strategy will probably cause an oversupply of memos. The last 1000 employees who receive memos will photocopy them only to find that there are no more people to give them to and about 2000 memos will end up in the trash. This is similar to what happens when animals like rabbits, mice and lemmings experience a massive population explosion only to find that there are insufficient resources to support them all and perish in vast numbers.

information to help the staff perform the duplication. Eve could have included a list or even a map of all photocopier locations to make sure that employees could find the closest one quickly. If she felt her colleagues were unfamiliar with the process of photocopying she could even have included instructions on how to operate the copier and where to find more paper if it ran out. As it is, Eve is confident that her colleagues know where the photocopier is and how to operate it. But this is not always the situation. People running critical operations, such as military commanders, tend to assume nothing and make sure that every possibility is taken into account. Let us just say for the moment that a set of self-replicating instructions may include information or *data* that will assist the recipient in carrying out the instructions.

The second element that Eve could have included is something to ensure that the instructions would be carried out. Eve might have been concerned about whether her colleagues will comply with the instructions in the memo. Since she has an executive position in the firm this is not likely to be a problem but if she were someone from outside the firm or a lower ranking employee she might have to provide some sort of incentive or coercion—a promise of reward or punishment.

At some stage, most people will have encountered the phenomenon known as chain letters. Chain letters usually ask the recipient to send copies of the letter to two or more other people. Recipients are often warned that calamity will befall them if they 'break the chain'. Often there is also a reward system. For example, the recipient is told to send a small sum of money to someone higher up the chain on the understanding that they in turn will receive many times that sum from people below them in the chain.

Although most people throw chain letters away, many dutifully pass them on in the vague fear that they might suffer some repercussions if they disobey the instructions. The people who initiate such letters can easily do a rough calculation of the percentage of letters likely to reach dead-ends and adjust the numbers of copies to be made in order to make a certain profit. In the same way, if Eve felt that a large number of employees were likely to discard her memo, she could have raised the number of copies to be made to three or four, in order to compensate.

Chain letters can be remarkably successful and can run for years, passing from country to country and making a lot of money for the people who are involved in the early stages at the expense of people who become involved later on. For this reason many countries have taken steps to ban them.

Eve's memo and chain letters, however, are examples of self-replicating systems operating in an environment without *rivals*. Things become more complicated when there are several self-replicating systems operating in the same population and competing for resources.

THE STORY OF ADAM

Adam Jones also works at Synaptic Systems. When he receives Eve's memo he reads it and, to his horror, sees what he thinks is an error in the announcement. He is anxious to correct the error but does not know how to do it since the memo is currently circulating through the company. He is in the middle of a meeting and does not have time to personally photocopy 2000 memos so decides to employ a similar strategy to Eve's. Adam prints out the following memo:

MEMO

To: All staff
From: Adam Jones

1. As soon as you receive this memo, photocopy it twice and give the copies to two colleagues who haven't seen it yet.
2. Retain this copy and read the announcement re meeting below.

> 3. Announcement re meeting:
>   A meeting of all staff is to be held in the auditorium
>   at 9:00 am on Tuesday, 6 June.
> 4. NOTE: This memo replaces the previous memo from
>   Eve re the meeting, which should be discarded.

Adam gives one copy of his memo to an associate and then returns to the meeting hoping that his strategy will work. What Adam does not know is that someone else is going to have the same idea.

THE STORY OF NOAH

Later that day Noah Brown receives both memos and reads them. His view is that both Adam's and Eve's announcements are wrong. He decides to issue a third memo with the following instructions:

MEMO

To: All staff
From: Noah Brown

1. As soon as you receive this memo, photocopy it twice and give the copies to two colleagues who haven't seen it yet.
2. Retain this copy and read the announcement re meeting below.
3. Announcement re meeting:
   A meeting of all staff is to be held in the auditorium at 9:00 am on Wednesday, 7 June.
4. NOTE: This memo replaces memos issued on this subject by Eve and Adam, which should BOTH be discarded.
   Only this memo is correct.

> If you are holding any copies of the memos issued by Eve and Adam please destroy them and do not copy or distribute them.

EVE'S RESPONSE

Meanwhile, in another city, Eve concludes a successful meeting with one of Synoptic's partner companies. She phones her office to set up a meeting on 6 June and is mystified to learn that this date clashes with the meeting that she announced in her memo. After a few more inquiries she is horrified to discover that that there are two other memos regarding the meeting circulating in competition with her own. From her laptop, she hastily prints out another copy of the original memo with an extra paragraph and faxes it to the office. The new memo reads:

URGENT MEMO

To: All staff
From: Eve Smith

1. As soon as you receive this memo, immediately make ten photocopies and give them to ten colleagues who haven't seen it yet.
2. Retain this copy and note the announcement re meeting below.
3. Announcement re meeting:
   A meeting of all staff is to be held in the auditorium at 9:00 am on Monday, 5 June.
4. PLEASE NOTE: Several memos regarding this matter are currently circulating. These should be discarded. This memo is the official memo in relation to this matter. To avoid confusion please do not copy or distribute any other memos on this subject and destroy any copies which may be in your possession.

> 5. Please make sure that everyone to whom you distribute this memo follows the instructions on it promptly.

Eve can do nothing now but hope that her memo spreads rapidly across the company and negates the other memos. But which memo will the staff believe to be the correct one?

Eve's second memo tells the staff to discard any other memos. However Adam's memo tells staff to ignore any memo issued by Eve while Noah's memo tells the staff to disregard memos issued by both Adam and Eve. To give her second memo a competitive edge, Eve has boosted the number of copies to be made from two to ten, hoping it will multiply faster than Noah's and Adam's, but will this work? Employees may resent having to make ten copies and distribute them. And what if the first person to read Eve's fax has just read either Adam's or Noah's memo, which both contain instructions to destroy *any* memo issued by Eve. If that person simply shreds the fax straightaway, Eve's second memo may never even get to the copying machine to start multiplying.

Eve has tried to make her second memo more compelling by wording it strongly and using words such as 'official' and 'immediately' in an attempt to convince the reader that this is the correct message. However, many employees may still think that this memo is the one that the other two memos have told them to destroy.

The number of people who make it to the meeting on 5 June will depend entirely on which memo is most effective at controlling the behaviour of the people in the Synaptic Systems office. Note that the result of the contest does not depend in any way on the *content* of the announcement but on how successful each memo is at orchestrating its own replication and overriding the other memos. This is the basic principle of tenetics.

CHAPTER 2

PROGRAMMING YOUR HUMAN BEING

ANOTHER WAY OF DESCRIBING the memos issued by Eve, Adam and Noah is to think of them as programs, a term that we now automatically associate with computers. Many people regard computers as glorified pocket calculators but there is one important difference.

A calculator is a machine that will add up and subtract. It will multiply and divide. It has buttons which are *hard wired* to perform these functions. The term *hard wired* is used because each button performs a specific function and will perform that function every time you press it. It performs those functions quickly and will continue to perform them as long as the power supply lasts. It will also perform these functions as soon as it is made. It comes off the assembly line fully operational and requires nothing more than a power supply—and a finger—to make it work. It also cannot be made to do anything more than it was designed to do.

A computer will perform all the functions of a calculator and many more. You can also use it to write text, draw a picture, play music or control a piece of machinery—it has a multitude of functions. However, it has none of these capabilities when it comes off the assembly line. It has a keyboard, a screen, some sort of storage device such as a hard drive and some memory chips where it can store information while the machine is switched on. But it will perform none of the functions listed above unless it is running the right programs.

A computer processor chip is like a microscopic railroad yard which marshals strings of electronic digits instead of trains. The chip switches those strings like a yard controller. It parks them on sidings while other 'trains' come through and then moves them off onto other sidings. It combines them with other strings and dispatches the result down the line to destinations in the memory chips with strange names like C000 or B2FF. It does all these things under the direction of a program called the operating system. The operating system (or OS) also controls the storage of the data on the disks, the output to the screen, communications over the Internet and so on. The chips do nothing but shove those little trains of digits around as directed.

We could say, if we wanted to draw a parallel between computers and animals, that a calculator has innate intelligence or instinct whereas a computer only attains the capacity to perform tasks when it is 'taught' what to do by loading a program into it.

Computer programs, like the memos proliferating on the desks at Synaptic Systems, are sequences of instructions that tell the computer what to do. Unless a computer has such a set of instructions to tell it what to do, it is no more than a pile of metal and silicon. Computers know so little, in fact, that computer programs have to supply the machine with everything it needs to know in order to perform a given task. Computer programmers (the people who write the instructions) must assume, like the commanders of critical operations, that the computer 'knows nothing'—which indeed it does—and that they must supply the machine with every conceivable piece of 'knowledge' it needs to carry out the instructions.

The result of this is that most computer programs are extremely long, consisting of millions of lines of instructions and data, all designed to guide the computer through complex operations. They are filled with 'if THIS, then THAT'-type branching instructions, which tell the computer what it should do upon receiving a certain input. They tell it how many times to perform operations and how to tell when the operation is finished. They contain error messages to flash when something goes wrong, help menus for the user, mathematical tables and formulae for converting data imported from other programs and so on. But not all computer programs are huge. In the 1980s, computer scientists at Massachusetts Institute of Technology (MIT) played a computer game called 'Core War'. 'Core War' was first described by A.K. Dewdney in *Scientific American* in May 1984. The field for the game is a 'virtual computer memory'—basically a long list (say 8000 lines) of instructions in which all the lines start off blank. The game is played by placing two 'warriors'—small programs—at random points in the list. Each line in the list is numbered but the warriors are not aware of the number of the line they are in. The list also 'wraps around' so that the end loops back to the beginning. The aim of the game is for one warrior to eradicate the other.

The simplest 'Core War' program consists of one line.

MOV 0, 1

This instruction means 'copy the instruction in line 0 (the current line) to line 1 (the next line along)'. When you execute this instruction it simply copies itself to the next line in the list. From there it will copy itself to the following line, and so on, until it goes right through the whole list, back to where it started. It will then continue to go round and round again till the game is stopped. If it catches up to the other warrior along the way, it will overwrite its instructions and eradicate it. Of course warrior 2 does not simply sit there waiting to be overwritten but moves ahead as well, trying to catch and overwrite warrior 1.

Since the computer executes instructions one at a time, each side taking turns, two warriors copying themselves forward one line at a time will never beat each other. Strategies have to be employed. The trick is to write a program that will multiply more efficiently or more ruthlessly than your opponent's.

Warriors can be written so they look forward till they find an address (line) that is not empty and then copy themselves into it. This is the equivalent of Adam issuing a memo which instructs staff to destroy any copies of Eve's memo. If Program A can locate the copy of Program B that is about to copy itself and erase it before it can do so, Program A effectively has the whole field to itself. Of course if Program B is jumping around randomly it might be quite hard for Program A to locate the active address of B. Warriors may also duplicate themselves so several clones of themselves are reproducing simultaneously. They may even set booby-traps so that any warrior creeping up 'behind' them is erased.

The warriors in 'Core War' and the strategies they employ clearly resemble the battling memos circulating around Synaptic Systems. They also strongly resemble what are referred to as computer viruses and in fact were the precursors of that phenomenon. A computer virus is simply a small self-replicating program that, once placed in the memory of a computer, continues to make copies of itself in the computer memory or on the computer's disks. Like the self-replicating memo and the chain letter, a computer virus contains instructions for its own duplication.

It is easy to see how computer viruses can be extremely destructive when they are released into the computers in the community. Viruses have the capacity to hide, undetected, in the memory of a computer and copy themselves onto floppy disks so that they will be transported to other computers where they can continue to replicate themselves. They may incorporate themselves surreptitiously into other programs or attach themselves to document files. They may even attach themselves to email messages and other Internet files so they can spread internationally.

To combat them, software companies have released anti-virus programs which 'hunt down' the viruses by looking for their characteristics and erase them from the memory and disks of the computer. Virus creators have in turn become more devious, writing viruses that hide themselves more efficiently or replicate more rapidly. Effectively there is an ongoing war between virus designers and anti-virus designers. The virus designers constantly strive to make their pesky products harder to detect and quicker to replicate; the anti-virus designers try harder and harder to outwit them.

Computer viruses, like Eve's memo, often contain messages. The more harmless of these simply display an announcement that the computer has been successfully infiltrated. The dangerous ones announce their presence by corrupting files, trashing the computer system, erasing the hard drive and so on. But like the Synaptic memos, the success of the virus has nothing to do with the message it conveys. Its ability to capture the computer depends on how well it can control the computer's functions, coexist with or even exploit other programs running on the computer and protect itself from anti-virus programs sent in to destroy it.

What I propose to show in this book is how the same thing happens in human society, how self-replicating programs spread through society by copying themselves into human minds and other storage devices. To begin with we need a brief overview of how the human brain—which like the computer comes off the assembly line with very little knowledge—is 'programmed' to be able to operate in the world.

Humans, unlike many other animals, are not born with in-built hard-wired programs that direct their behaviour. We certainly have reflexes and drives that are necessary to ensure our survival but we are not able to automatically perform complex sequences of actions the way a bird builds a nest or spider builds a web: we have to *learn*. On the other hand, our capacity for learning is enormous. Like the computer, we may not have the simplicity and reliability of the hand calculator, but we make up for it by being *programmable*.

THE WORLD PICTURE

We humans carry in our heads a vast amount of information, most of which we take on trust. Very few people have the time or resources to personally test all the propositions[1] that are put to them every day. We do not all have laboratories, observatories, microscopes or oceanic exploration vessels. We do not run our own news-gathering services, survey organisations or statistics bureaus. Throughout our lives we depend mainly on received knowledge to form our view of the world and the only way we can tell whether this received knowledge is reliable or not is by comparing it with our own experience, taking into account the opinions of others and making some judgement about the reliability of the person who is communicating it.[2]

Whether we regard a proposition as 'true' or not will depend on whether it fits into our *World Picture*—our own perception of what is true or real. Most of us are not aware of having a picture of the world as such. It seems that the world is simply out there, around us, and we are here looking at it, until we talk to others and read other people's accounts of their lives, particularly people from different countries and cultures. Then we are often struck by how differently other people see things. Sometimes it is as if they lived in a separate universe. However, generally, we do not believe that the universe is actually different for different people.

---

1   By 'proposition' I mean anything that purports to be a statement of fact such as 'The prime minister resigned today' or 'I like pizza'.

2   Our view of the person transmitting the knowledge is most important and may explain why newsreaders who can deliver the news with a sense of authority—that is, they are believable—are among the most highly paid people in the media.

What we assume is that everyone sees the world differently. We all have different World Pictures.

Although there are differences between everybody's World Picture, people generally require their own World Picture to have internal consistency, which means that it should not contain obvious contradictions. We cannot, for example, simultaneously believe that the day after Monday is Tuesday and that the day before Tuesday is Sunday. Propositions must agree with each other or the World Picture will fail in its purpose of helping us to make confident predictions. Our World Picture is our roadmap and instruction manual for living in our surroundings. It provides us with assurances that the sun will rise tomorrow, that there are 100 cents in the dollar and if you let go of a glass over a tile floor it will fall and probably break. When a proposition is presented that contradicts the elements of our picture it is likely to cause confusion and anxiety.

Challenging someone's World Picture may result in outright hostility or violence as many scientists and social reformers have discovered over the years when they tried to promote concepts such as a spherical earth, evolution, relativity, the unconscious mind and racial equality. The extreme emotional reaction to some of these concepts demonstrates how important it is for people to feel that their World Picture is accurate and consistent. By accurate I mean that to the best of our belief our World Picture represents *objective reality*. Being consistent means that as far as we can see, all the propositions in our World Picture are compatible with each other. The limitations here are, of course, the words 'to the best of our belief' and 'as far as we can see'. Those limitations have far-reaching consequences.

BUILDING A WORLD PICTURE

The process by which people acquire their view of the world and the ability to operate in that world is called *learning*. Learning happens automatically in just about every creature that possesses a nervous system. From the moment a young animal comes into the world it begins to learn. Human societies go further. They do not simply rely on infants learning by themselves but take steps to see that children learn what adults think they ought to learn. This is called *education*.

Learning has become a value-laden word. Traditionally is has been equated with 'wisdom' or 'enlightenment'. It tends to mean 'learning what we believe to be true'. Thus, if we speak of a 13th century Hindu child *learning* that the earth is a flat disk supported by four elephants on the back of a giant turtle, many people will say that is not learning at all, because *it is not true*. Yet the Hindu child is undergoing a learning process just as much as the child who is taught that the earth is a ball revolving around the sun. Learning is simply the acquisition of skills and the development of a World Picture.

The World Picture is central to the idea of learning and thinking. It is no accident that a vast amount of research into learning has been based on psychologists teaching rats to run mazes. Countless experiments have shown that rats, cats, mice, even earthworms, can learn to find their way through a maze. Animals with even the simplest neural systems appear to be able to hold a 'map' of a maze in their brain—or whatever clump of neurons serves as a brain. Whether they 'picture' the maze as a two-dimensional pattern, or whether they simply remember a set of rules such as left, right, right, left, right, left, left, we cannot tell but such memories form and appear to be able to persist over time.

It is not hard to understand why some sort of geographical picture is necessary for an animal that moves through its environment. To be able to find food and water and then return to its den, nest or hive, an animal clearly needs some sort of internal spatial map or navigation strategy. A baby crawling around the house quickly forms a mental map of the home. By the time they are walking most children know their way around their own house. They know where their toys and books are kept and even in which drawers certain clothes are. They are also aware of the other places that exist beyond the home, such as 'the playground', 'the park' or 'Grandma's' though they may have no idea of how far or in which direction these places are.

As they grow, children also become aware of certain rules that exist in the world. They learn that certain things make Mummy or Daddy angry. They learn that dropping things may break them, that certain foods taste good or bad and that certain things are to be feared. As new experiences and information are received each day, their World Picture slowly pieces together like a jigsaw. The child gains a sense of what we call *reality*. This view of reality needs frequent modification.

A child who sees a story about lions on television may fear that such creatures could be roaming in their vicinity. The parent modifies the World Picture by explaining, 'There are no lions around here. They live in Africa, a long way away.' This instruction imparts several concepts. It not only modifies the child's beliefs in relation to lions, it also introduces another place called Africa which is 'a long way away'. This introduces two new concepts into the child's World Picture:

1. There are places that are a long way away.
2. Different animals live in different places.

Thus the World Picture grows and is constantly refined and reshaped. Parents sometimes deliberately manipulate the child's World Picture, for example, by telling the child that if they're not good, Santa won't bring them any Christmas presents. The parent knows there is no Santa but is aware that the child is likely to believe what the parent says and incorporate into their reality a rule to the effect: 'Bad behaviour = no toys'. The child accepts the parents' story about Santa for two obvious reasons:

1. The proposition does not contradict any existing concepts in their world.
2. Since Mum and Dad have taught them pretty much everything they know up to this point, their word carries a fair bit of weight.

It is worth pointing out that such acceptance does not imply any weakness of intellect on the child's part and that, as adults, we too are just as likely to accept a proposition put to us by a highly respected source that we have no reason to doubt.

THEORIES AND MODELS

The scientific terms for a World Picture are 'theory' or 'model'. Just as a model plane or a model ship is the likeness of a real object, a scientific model attempts to be a representation of reality. It is a tentative image of a system that helps people envisage how the system works. A model can be a three-dimensional object such as those collections of wire and coloured balls that purport to represent molecules or it can be a computer program written to emulate weather patterns or ocean currents. There are models of magnetic fields, population growth, the movement of continents and stock market activity.

The thing scientists acknowledge is that models—and in fact all theories—are works in progress. Physical, biological and social scientists use models to generate predictions that they can check against actual events through experiment or research. If the outcome of the experiments or the research matches the predictions, then the model is felt to be confirmed for the time being. The model may then be extended and tested further. However, as soon as the observed events don't match the predictions, it is back to the drawing board for at least some part of the model.

All of what we think of as science and knowledge is in fact a series of models. We have models for the internal structure of the nucleus of the atom, the interiors of stars, the Big Bang, biological evolution, the behaviour of objects in motion, clouds and the human mind. Some of these models are contentious and subject to continual modification. Others have concurred with observed events for so long that they have come to be regarded as *axiomatic*, something that seems to be unquestionably true. And yet from time to time someone will come across a phenomenon that even an established model cannot explain.

Isaac Newton's formulation of the laws of physics was held for hundreds of years to be the ultimate model of how the universe worked. That was until late in the 19th century when certain astronomical and electromagnetic phenomena were discovered which seemed to 'break the rules'. Enter the Theory of Relativity, courtesy of Albert Einstein, not a refutation of Newton, but an add-on to explain the behaviour of matter and energy in dimensions larger and at speeds faster than those that Newton had been able to observe. At the same time Max Planck devised a model for the behaviour of sub-atomic particles called Quantum Theory, which set out to explain why the universe appeared not to obey Newton at the microscopic scale.

Interestingly, Relativity Theory and Quantum Theory initially seemed to contradict each other but over the 20th century have become much more integrated. This takes us back to the issue of internal consistency. Scientific models— like the components of our personal World Pictures—not only have to be supported by events observed in the real world, they also must be—in the final analysis—compatible with *each other*. It would be a very confusing situation if two models seemed to agree absolutely with the facts—that is, every experiment that was carried out seemed to support both models—and yet the models contradicted each other, as seemed to be the case with Quantum Theory and Relativity. Sooner or later one or both of the models would have to be modified so that they can both become part of a larger model—the overall World Picture.

That is what has happened, and continues to happen, in

human knowledge since the beginning of history. Gradually all the different models join together to make one gigantic model—the Theory of Everything—which, to some people, is the goal of science. Whether such a goal is possible will become clearer as we move on.

To give an example of converging models: for centuries geneticists explored the behaviour of genes without being able to see them. Pioneer geneticists studied the way in which the characteristics of flowers or animals were passed on to their progeny by observing the outcomes of breeding. From these observations, although they could not *see* the active mechanism, they derived certain laws and principles. Later on molecular biologists began studying the structure of reproductive cells and their behaviour. In the 1950s these two models came together with the identification and description of the DNA molecule, the molecule that splits in half and combines with *another* DNA molecule to create a new individual. From then on, the model for genetics and the model for cellular processes were fused into one all-encompassing model for reproduction, which covers the process from the atomic level right up to outcomes in living populations.

However complex this process of formulating, testing and modifying models sounds, it is basically the same thing that is going on in the mind of a three-year-old child.

THE ROLE OF LANGUAGE

As children grow, they are continually adding to and modifying their model of the world. Like the European explorers who expanded their maps of the known world by successive voyages into perilous waters, children add to their maps of the universe. To the map of the home and the yard is added the map of the street, the pre-school, friends' houses, the shops, the park and the playground. This world is populated initially with Mummy and/or Daddy, and brothers and sisters. To these are added, in time, relatives, neighbours, child-minders, teachers, and other adults and children.

The child soon perceives that other families have relationships and members similar to their own. They also notice that buildings have similar features—doors, windows, furniture—and that animals also have similar properties—heads, legs, tails and so on. This recognition and identification of common elements in the world is both aided and directed by the learning of language. As the child encounters phenomena the parents name those phenomena, thereby imposing onto the child's direct experience a *classification* of phenomena, a set of categories into which things are grouped. The first animal a child ever sees may be a dog. Thereafter the child may call all four-legged creatures 'dog' until the parents point out that the animals are in fact called 'cat' or 'cow'.

What is important to note here is that this process of categorisation often requires the child to substantially ignore their own perceptions and 'natural' reactions. For example, the child will learn that the door of a house and the door of a car, though they are different shapes and materials, are in the same category, while a sheet of white drawing paper and the white living-room wall, which may seem to a child to be substantially the same, are placed in vastly different categories. They will learn that a Pekinese and a Great Dane, while looking utterly different, are both dogs while a Pekinese dog and a Persian cat, which look similar, are labelled differently.[3]

These experiences teach the child an important thing: the reasons for classification can be 'hidden'. The Pekinese and the Great Dane are classified as 'dog' because of genetic similarities which the child has to take 'on authority' because they are not directly visible. Thus the child learns that

---

3   While the adults seem to be obviously 'right' in this example, taxonomy (species labelling) can be very tricky and biologists can have great trouble deciding exactly in which family a creature should be placed.

sometimes they must subordinate their own criteria for classification to a system that is dictated to them by their parents and teachers.

For adults these classifications are 'natural' and adults see themselves as imparting the 'truth' about these matters to the child. However, labels are not absolute, they are 'constructs' that are imposed by society for specific reasons.

As a simple example, consider that, in the English-speaking world, electric saws, electric drills and electric heat-guns are classified as 'tools' but electric knives, electric mixers and electric hair dryers are called 'appliances'. Even though these machines work on precisely the same principles and, in the case of the heat-gun and the hair dryer, look almost identical, the items mainly used by men are referred to as 'tools' while the items more often used by women are called 'appliances'. Language is used to maintain the illusion that men are primarily the tool-users in society even though women, who still do the bulk of the cooking, washing and cleaning, use a large array of mechanical equipment.

The most important labels are those attached to people and behaviour.

Classifying certain acts as 'naughty' or 'good' can obviously have long-lasting effects on the World Picture of a child and classifying people into categories—black and white, Catholic and Protestant, left-wing and right-wing, gay and straight, Aryan and Jewish can eventually lead to savage social conflicts and even genocide. Many violent ethnic conflicts (Tutsi and Hutu, Bosnian and Serb) are characterised by a belief on both sides that their opponents are fundamentally a different class of being from themselves. Even when there is no physical difference between the warring factions, children can be raised to believe that, even though the people in the neighbouring province look the same, they have 'hidden differences' that set them apart. Sometimes these differences are identified as doctrinal, but they are more often characterised as racial—in other words genetic—usually where no such genetic difference actually exists.

The result is that, by imposing certain categories on a child, cultures predispose the child toward certain moral, intellectual, political, even scientific beliefs in adult life. In this sense language does not simply reflect our sense of reality, it actually creates it.

The important point is that whatever difficulty the child may have in understanding the way things are labelled and grouped, in the end the child will most likely adopt the system that the adults have imposed. It's simply a matter of survival. There are penalties for not knowing the rules which is why the first day at a new school and the first day at a new job can be very stressful. The purpose of the World Picture is to help us function without making mistakes. It is there to help us to achieve what we want to do without suffering physical harm or falling into conflict with other people.

Because we need a sense of reliability in our perceptions of things, a lack of consistency in the World Picture can be devastating for an individual. Clinical psychologists have postulated that children who are continually given conflicting rules can develop deep insecurity and can suffer mental disturbance as adults. Children are continually encountering what appear to be contradictions in the world and must continually modify their World Picture to try and maintain a sense of overall consistency. For example, children who have been encouraged to express themselves at home may get into trouble for laughing and talking at school. The solution comes when the child realises that there are different sets of rules for home and at school. Later on, the same child will expand this realisation to learn that there are different rules for behaviour at home and when out visiting or among peers and that there are even different rules for behaviour between different peer groups.

What the child has learned is that there are rules *about* rules. This development helps stabilise the World Picture by explaining contradictions and helping us cope in a greater variety of situations. At the same time it presents a threat to the system of belief that the parents have imposed because having 'rules about rules' is only a short step away from 'thinking about thinking'.

ALTERNATIVE WORLD PICTURES

As children grow up, some sections of the World Picture tend to suffer compatibility problems with the rest. For example, while young children have no difficulty believing in Santa Claus, as they grow older the idea can begin to conflict with other information they are receiving. The logistics of one person delivering presents to all the children in the world in one night starts to look a bit daunting and it starts to become increasingly obvious that parents are principally involved in present buying. By a certain age, if they have not been told, many children will independently begin to question the reality of Santa Claus. This does not mean however that children would, if not told outright, automatically abandon the belief.

It is important to realise that, while compatibility problems in belief systems can raise questions, they do not automatically lead to abandonment of belief. It all depends on how the incompatibility is explained. An imaginative parent could probably keep their children convinced of the existence of Santa Claus well into their adolescence if they kept making the explanations more sophisticated—in keeping with the child's increased level of knowledge. Thus, problems of inconsistency can be dealt with by adding *more concepts* to the World Picture, to account for the apparent contradictions. This may sound clumsy and unworkable but it is the method by which many scientific theories are kept operating. It is also the way in which our system of law is maintained with judges and legislators constantly making new findings and passing new Bills to deal with inconsistencies created by the existing ones.

Of course the parents' attempt to maintain the Santa Claus myth would only work if nothing was mentioned by other children which leads us to an important factor in the construction of the child's World Picture: the influence of the peer group.

The construction of reality is a task in which children actively co-operate with each other. Children are very quick to impart knowledge ('Do you know what? . . .' 'Guess what I just found out . . .') and to modify the perceptions of others ('That's not how you do it!'). Knowledge is important to children. They are anxious to learn about the nature of the world and their own place in it and they look to other children to enhance that knowledge. They are impatient with other children who do not know what they themselves know ('Don't you know anything?') and can become enraged with a child who maintains a view to the contrary of their own views. Failure to know what you are supposed to know, or worse, to believe something you are not supposed to believe can lead to conflict or ostracism from the group with considerable unhappiness as a result. Hence, early in the piece, children have to reconcile a World Picture that has been imparted to them by their parents and teachers with one espoused by other children. As parents and teachers know, the peer-group view frequently wins.

Part of the power of the peer group comes from the fact that at a certain age children start to learn that adults are capable of manipulating information in their own interest. Because of their custodial role and the need to instil discipline and preserve decorum, parents and teachers can be seen as having no hesitation in distorting matters when it suits them. Adults will often tell children that they cannot do things or have things because 'You wouldn't like it', 'It's too dangerous', 'It's too far' or 'We can't afford it'. While these reasons are accepted in the early years, as they grow older, many children begin to suspect that some of these statements might not turn out to be completely true were they submitted to further scrutiny. The children will then endeavour to test such propositions by approaching them from different angles, for example, 'But I already tried and I did like it' or 'I asked my friend and she said it's not dangerous'. They also may start applying tests: 'Angela is allowed to so why can't I?'. In these cases parents may have no choice but to abandon their mild distortion of the facts and simply rely on the debate-stopping line of 'Because I say so'. These sorts of exchanges then produce in the child the realisation that parental statements of 'fact' can sometimes be influenced by the parent's own feelings and interests.

The irony is that the distinction between 'true' and 'untrue' statements is one of the first concepts that parents teach children. Parents teach the concept of truth and falsehood to children when they are very young to protect them from being told lies, confusing fantasy with reality and telling lies themselves. Of course at that stage it is implicit that statements made by the parents are the truth. It is inevitable, however, that in time the child will apply these rules of truthfulness to the parents' own utterances.

This process is abetted by the child's growing awareness that some people have significantly different World Pictures from their parents. As children mix with other children they usually become aware that other families have slightly different rules from their own, though these are usually nothing too dramatic. They may simply be different rules for household behaviour, regarding the consumption of certain foods or use of language. Sometimes, however, the child may encounter a set of rules and behaviours that are radically different from those that operate within their own family. This raises the tantalising suspicion that it may be possible to transgress the principles imposed by their parents, and still operate efficiently and happily in the world.

The probability of children encountering World Pictures significantly different from their own and the way they react to them when they do depends on a number of factors.

If a child has been raised in a highly controlled or homogeneous society—what we call a monoculture—such encounters are less likely in the short term. For example, a child raised in a family that belongs to a certain church, and is sent to a church school and only allowed to associate with the children of other church members, may take some time to meet people whose belief systems are different from their own. When they do, those beliefs and behaviours are most likely to be met with hostility or fear. However, children living in more diverse societies, who attend government schools and are allowed to mix freely with others will become aware at an early age that other families and individuals have quite different belief systems. They will become aware that people value different commodities, support different political parties, observe different moral codes, follow different customs in relation to marriage and child rearing and, most of all, hold vastly diverging beliefs regarding the creation, the structure and the governance of the universe. The child in other words starts to 'think about thinking'.

Whatever their background, as children move out into the world (or the world moves in on them via television, magazines, radio, music and the Internet) they will be exposed to a range of influences that will tend to modify their World Picture including (though not limited to) commercially constructed youth culture, delinquent subcultures, and religious and political cults.

Commercially constructed youth culture

Commercially constructed youth culture is the product of business interests intent on fostering young people as a consumer market. It grew to prominence after the Second World War when businesses in affluent Western societies identified 'teenagers' as a new emerging consumer category and set about designing and manufacturing products for this market. The transformation of children into independent consumer 'units' has now extended down in age to preschool children in a process of global youth marketing. It is not my intention to go into the mechanisms of this process here. Suffice it to say that businesses that target young people as consumers rely heavily on identifying their products with concepts of generational identity.

The general strategy is to appeal to the young person's quest for identity by challenging 'old fashioned' (that is, the parents') values and reinforcing the young person's sense of individuality and independence. Hence marketing slogans emphasise concepts along the lines of 'Do your own thing', 'No one can tell you what to do', 'Today', 'Because you're you' and so on, which cater to the child's desire to see themselves as free from adult influences.

Of course, these commercially constructed campaigns do not attempt to challenge the young person's fundamental beliefs but focus mainly on cultural elements such as clothes, diet, make-up, music, films, games, pastimes and social activities. They are, after all, trying to sell clothes and soft drinks, not political revolution, so their aim is only to change those elements of the teenager's World Picture that affect *purchasing* behaviour, not the fundamental tenets of belief. The paradox is, of course, that while promoting the concept of independent thought and 'doing your own thing' the aim of the merchandisers is really just the opposite: to induce the adolescent to conform to a global trend in purchasing a massproduced item.

In creating the myth of rebellion and individualism, the creators of commercial culture exploit another category of influence: delinquent subculture, from which they draw ideas that are then presented in a harmless context. An example of this is the spate of teenage 'rebel' films made in the 1950s—*Rebel Without a Cause*, *The Wild One* and so on. In the unified culture of the fifties, the notion of a young person breaking the rules of society was an intriguing one. The concept of living outside the rules of Western suburbia has continued to be explored and exploited by the punk and heavy metal bands of the seventies, eighties and nineties. These entertainment products present models of transgressional behaviour and attitudes in a relatively non-threatening way so they can be experienced vicariously by the young audience. That is to say, the young people watching the film or concert do not necessarily actually engage in the behaviours illustrated. They do not necessarily join motorcycle gangs, defy all authority or indulge in unrestrained hedonistic behaviour. Instead they engage in these activities in their imaginations. The young target market may even seek to extend the experience of watching the film or the rock concert by dressing like their heroes in real life. Thus in the fifties, young men might adopt a James Dean or an Elvis Presley hairstyle, in the nineties they might dress like Marilyn Manson. This is simply a way of continuing the vicarious experience of independence and rebellion beyond the doors of the concert hall or outside the private world of their own imagination. Though commercially constructed youth culture can give parents many sleepless nights, the true delinquent subculture is of much more real concern.

Delinquent subcultures

The child who is going through the process of doubting their parents' value system can easily be influenced by a peer group with an 'anti-authority' culture. This culture may praise people for smoking, taking drugs, shoplifting, certain kinds of sexual behaviour, stealing cars, burglary or violence. The peer group dismisses the values of the adult world by simply declaring teachers, parents, police and other adult figures to be *the enemy*.

THE RETURN OF EVE

When Eve returned to the office after her trip she was determined to avoid another debacle similar to the one that occurred while she was away. So she circulated the following memo by the normal methods:

MEMO

To: All staff
From: Eve Smith

A few days ago a considerable amount of confusion was created by contradictory memos circulating in the office. To avoid this happening in future please note that from this date onwards the only memos to be acted on are those issued by myself.

All memos issued by other persons are to be disregarded and destroyed.

Signed
Eve Smith

What Eve has done in the name of efficiency, and to assert her own authority, is to try to create a permanent lock-out by instructing the staff to disregard communications from other sources. This final memo sets out to discredit, and strip of any sense of authority, any memo issued by another person.

The question now arises: if Adam or Noah wish to circulate a memo on any topic, how can they break the lock-out? It is no use issuing memos as any memo from them will probably be disregarded even if it is a memo telling staff to disregard Eve's memo. They cannot call staff to a meeting to discuss the issue because any memo announcing a meeting (unless it is issued by Eve) will be disregarded.

THE LOCK-OUT

A World Picture that includes the idea of 'adults as enemy' can easily make sense to a child or adolescent who has experienced disappointment and suffering at the hands of adults—or a demanding individual who suddenly finds they can't get their own way. Betrayal of trust, telling lies, imposing restrictions and acts of self-interest by adults can all add credibility to this view of the world. In some cases, anti-authoritarian views are inculcated in children from birth. Children raised in families that exist within a criminal sub-culture are raised to believe that police and other authorities are the enemy, a belief that will be reinforced if they see police coming to the house to arrest their parents or seeing family members incarcerated. This can lead to a firm belief that life is a battle between the Authorities and the Victimised Battlers. The aim of life is to get away with disobeying authority as much as you can without getting caught.

Of course when teachers, parents and police do catch the child and punish them, it only serves to reinforce the existing view that this is a war and the authority figures are the other side.

This creates great difficulties in modifying the behaviour of delinquent subcultures. Punishing members of the sub-culture only *confirms* their belief that authority figures are against them (which, of course, to a great extent they are). The delinquents' reaction is not to change their behaviour but to try harder not to get caught next time. At the same time, attempts to reason with the members of the subculture are likely to be met with mistrust. Members of the subculture tend to regard efforts by authorities to appear kind and under-standing as simply a *trick* by the enemy. The result is that members of delinquent subcultures not only mistrust figures such as police officers but also people such as social workers, teachers, counsellors, psychologists and doctors. This is because their World Picture contains a lock-out provision, just like the one in Eve's memo, which warns them to disregard any-thing said by, for example, middle class people or authorities.

The drug subculture systematises this kind of lock-out by labelling everyone who is not a illicit drug user as a 'straight', a term with vaguely, if not distinctly, pejorative overtones. It is the straights that have the 'problem' with drugs, not the users, that problem being a narrow-mindedness about drugs that is the result of them, well, being straights. The implication is that straights don't understand; straights have not discovered the 'secret' of drugs yet, so it is no use confiding in a straight and you can never trust a straight.

Counsellors and social workers working with people from delinquent subcultures continually face this problem of being locked-out. In fact the lock-out is one of the most common characteristics of social conflict. Ardent trade unionists will approach labour negotiations from the assumption that employers—as members of the capitalist class—can *never* be trusted. Business people will have the same view of the unionists. White racists will mistrust people of different skin colours, black power groups will think the worst of the white establishment.

Religious and political cults

The third form of influence on young people has the potential to create the most widespread concern. The difference between the delinquent subculture and political or religious cults lies in the sophistication of the lock-out mechanisms. The tenets of a delinquent subculture are likely to be the result of certain values being transmitted in childhood or the result of some subsequent alienation from adult authority figures. They may go no further than such attitudes as 'All cops are bastards' or 'All teachers are bastards'.

Religious and political movements, on the other hand, reinforce their tenets with far more credible 'evidence' that lends a feeling of intellectual objectivity and authenticity to their propositions. Typically, political and religious movements that are outside the mainstream beliefs of society will, like the members of delinquent subcultures, label the views of parents and teachers as 'wrong'—though in much more elaborated terms.[4]

---

4   A disturbing facet of the counterculture of the late 1960s in the USA was the way members of the criminal subculture infiltrated the hippie movement. Middle-class teenagers mingled unguardedly with dangerous sociopaths because they too expressed anti-authoritarian sentiments.
A well-known and tragic example was Charles Manson who used bizarre stories of an impending race war to convert a group of teenage runaways into a death-squad.

Radical left-wing organisations may tell young people that their parents are typical conservative, middle-class people who are part of the machinery of capitalist oppression and so on. They might substantiate such views with historical material showing the centuries-old oppression of the working class by the bourgeoisie, and texts that demonstrate how society could be improved by the adoption of radical changes. Of course they will tell their followers to disregard opinions expressed by opponents of such changes because those people have been 'brainwashed by the system' and 'cannot see the truth'. Ironically, they may also state, as I have above, that reality is a construct of language in order to discredit the prior knowledge that the young person has acquired.

At the same time, radical right-wing groups may tell young people that their society, including the government, their teachers, the policy makers and the media, have all become pawns in a conspiracy to subvert the sovereignty of the national government and subjugate it to an inter-national—usually Marxist—conspiracy. Reform movements such as feminism, conservation, gay rights and gun control are all seen as facets of this conspiracy. Again, they might emphasise the idea that people cannot trust what they read and hear in the media because the communications industry is all *part* of the conspiracy and they, the leaders of the movement, are the only ones who can be trusted. Once more we see a classic lock-out strategy designed to negate any contradictory information coming from the rest of the world.

Religious cults almost invariably tell young people that people outside the cult are 'blind to the truth' while those within the cult have 'seen the light'. They often demand that recruits to the cult throw off the beliefs imparted to them by their parents and adopt a whole new value and belief system. Parents are naturally hurt and confused when their children suddenly announce that they are rejecting the principles with which they have been raised and are adopting a new set of beliefs—a new World Picture. Parents can be particularly distressed when their children accuse them of being arch-conservatives, pawns, bigots, idiots or—in extreme cases—child-molesters.

Sometimes when their children have joined religious cults parents will hire people to get them back. These people, who are specialists in dealing with people who have joined such cults, describe their task as *de-programming* the young people. It is important to understand that the term *de-programming* is not a metaphor.

Religions and other belief systems *are* programs, and systems for negating them, like anti-virus software, are also programs. These programs compete with each other by using certain strategies that are common to all self-replicating systems. We will now look at these universal strategies and see just how complicated and powerful they can become.

CHAPTER 3

LIVING BY THE CODE

IF WE LOOK AT the memos in the Synaptic Systems story we can see that, to succeed, a self-replicating program must possess certain features and perform certain functions.

1. *Coding.* The instructions must be expressed in a form that can be communicated and understood. In the case of the memos, the instructions are coded in English, the language that all the employees at Synaptic speak and understand.

2. *Embodiment.* The program must create or find some sort of physical manifestation in which it can reside in order to be stored and communicated. Eve's memos were printed on pieces of paper. Other forms of embodiment were possible. Eve could have *told* someone the message before she left the building and said 'Pass it on'. In that case embodiment of the code would have been in a series of sounds—verbal utterances. This is, however, not a particularly durable embodiment. If the listener hears the message, walks into their office and then stops and thinks '*What* did she say I had to do?' the process of replication could halt.

3. *Embedding*. The instructions for reproducing the code must be contained within the code itself. Eve's memo includes the instructions for duplication at the top of the page. Since they are on the same page as the message there is little chance of them being separated. Consider the risk if Eve had issued the announcement on a covering sheet separate from the instructions for copying. There is good chance that somewhere down the line an employee might pass on the announcement but not the instructions. Like a cell without DNA, the announcement would be valid but 'sterile', that is—not capable of reproducing. Note, however, that if Eve had put the instructions and the announcement on separate sheets and someone lost the announcement sheet, the instruction sheet would probably continue to be photocopied and distributed—even though it was meaningless—because it contains the self-replication code.

4. *Activation*. The code must contain instructions that cause a reaction in the surrounding environment. Eve activates her memo by typing 'Memo; To: All staff' etc. on the top. If she did not do this her memo would be just a piece of paper and there would be no reason for anyone to obey the instructions in it. Eve knows that the employees of the firm will usually act on the instructions contained in an official memo. The purpose of the heading is to cause a physical action on the part of the employees. They must walk to the photocopier, put the memo in and press the button. The memo cannot reproduce by itself. It has to harness the physical energy of a human being. As we will see, all self-replicating programs must find and exploit a source of energy.

5. *Resource management*. The memo also contains instructions that control its efficiency. Eve's memo specifies that the employees must copy the document 'as soon' as they receive it. It also specifies the number of copies to be made. As discussed previously, these elements can be

critical in a competitive situation. Had the memo instructed the employee to make the copy 'as soon as possible'
or 'when you get a moment' or 'within 24 hours' the
rival memos of Adam and Noah would rapidly have
overtaken it. In the second memo that Eve circulated she
raised the number of copies to be made. This tactic not
only increases the number of copies in circulation, it may
confer another advantage: people copying Adam and
Noah's memos might be slowed down if the people
copying Eve's are spending longer at the photocopier.
In a competitive environment tactics affecting the utilis-
ation of time and resources can be critical to the survival
of the system.

6. *Defence.* Eve's memo instructs staff to disregard and
destroy any other memos competing for their attention.
Since the other memos circulating tell staff to destroy
Eve's memo she must try to get in first.

7. *Reproduction.* The memo instructs staff to photocopy the
memo and distribute it. We know from point 3 that the
instructions for reproduction are embedded in the memo.

8. *Nurturing.* In her second memo Eve adds a final instruction that employees should ensure that the people they
give copies to actually do copy it and pass it on. This is
a kind of double check to make sure the system is
working.

SELF-REPLICATING MOLECULES

The preceding steps are common to all self-replicating systems. In the biological world they might work something
like this:

1. *Coding.* Genetic instructions are coded as a series of
amino acids.

2. *Embodiment.* The DNA is embodied as the long spiral
called a DNA molecule. This molecule, however, when

activated, builds an organism around it, let's say a fox. This extended body has mobility, ingestion, perception and information-processing facilities.

3. *Embedding.* Every cell in the fox's body contains a copy of the same DNA code.

4. *Activation.* The fox has drives such as hunger which causes it to hunt other creatures, eat them, digest them and use the energy derived to continue moving, eating, digesting and so on. It will also feel fear, which causes it to avoid dangerous situations, and a desire to mate.

5. *Resource management.* The fox has a number of characteristics that make it a competitive biological 'machine'. It can run fast, dig holes and carry prey substantial distances. It hunts methodically around its territory. It eats meat, which provides more energy per gram than, for example, vegetation. It has a fur coat that reduces heat-loss. It drives other foxes out of its territory.

6. *Defence.* The fox is equipped with sharp teeth, acute eyesight and good hearing. It hunts at night and sleeps in the daytime. It digs a burrow in which to conceal itself and its cubs.

7. *Reproduction.* The fox will mate with another fox thereby combining its DNA with the mate and building another set of foxes.

8. *Nurturing.* The female fox feeds the cubs with her milk and guards them until they are old enough to protect themselves. She will also subsequently teach the cubs to hunt.

To summarise in the simplest terms, a successful biological self-replicating system needs a list of coded instructions, a physical entity in which the code can reside, access to energy, the capacity to defend itself, the ability to reproduce and in some cases the ability to nurture its progeny.

Its performance of all this tasks—and note that these elements include behaviours as well as physical features—will determine its success as a 'replicator'. But how do these requirements apply to something as abstract as ideas? To answer this I will address each of the basic requirements of a self-replicating system and see how they manifest themselves in human thought.

CODING

To begin with, at heart, *all* self-replicating systems including computer viruses and the DNA molecule are abstract. It is not the physical cluster of objects but the set of instructions that cause the self-replication to occur. These instructions are coded in a form that will trigger some change in the physical environment. A computer program consists of instructions that are 'understood' by a computer: these instructions put the chips in the computer memory into certain states.

Computer programs are written in *lines* of code. DNA molecules consist of a sequence of molecules called *codons* (because they spell out the chemical code) joined into a giant molecule. Belief systems, which I will call *doctrines*, are also made up of units, which I will call *tenets*. Tenets are basically propositions—what we commonly refer to as statements of fact or belief. They are the building blocks of our World Picture and our shared culture. In the Judeo-Christian religions the Ten Commandments and the elements of Mosaic law might be regarded as tenets. In the politics of the United States, the articles of the constitution might be regarded as the tenets of the system. The axioms of Euclid might be regarded as tenets of geometry.

These propositions, however, cannot be transmitted in an abstract form. Like Eve's memo, they must have a physical manifestation (embodiment). In human beings, tenets are manifested in the form of neural connections in the brain. Whether we regard them as 'memories', 'facts', 'concepts' or 'learned responses', they are physical features of the cortex. In order to communicate these tenets from one brain to another they have to be coded in a form that human brains can understand. That code is called language.

Just as a the instructions in a computer program put the computer into a certain state, language may be generally taken to be a set of sounds, symbols or images that put the human mind into a certain state. That state may involve the existence of certain images in the mind of the recipient, an alteration of the recipient's memory structures or some behaviour on the part of the recipient. The language may be oral, it may be written, it may be recorded, but it is through language that the tenets of all our doctrines are communicated be they rules and regulations, scientific theories, everyday observations, political theories, economic theories, religious faiths, government policies or just gossip.

The simplest example of communication by language is someone telling something to someone else and that person passing it on. We can describe this somewhat mechanically as:

- A certain configuration of neurons and electro-chemical activity exists in the brain of Person 1.
- Person 1 codes that configuration as a series of vocal utterances which Person 2 hears.
- Person 2's brain decodes those sounds and forms new nerve connections that in some way resemble the connections in Person 1's brain.
- Person 2 now translates the same idea into another set of verbal noises directed at Person 3.

Notice here that the idea has changed its embodiment several times. It has started off as a configuration of neurons, been translated into a pattern of sound waves, been translated back into a pattern of neurons and then back into sound waves again.

This sounds very simple, but it represents an extraordinary evolutionary leap for living, learning creatures. The ability of humans to copy their cognitive structures from person to person represents one of the most dramatic developments in the history of the world. Before the evolution of language, the behaviour of living creatures could only be determined by three things: instinct, imitation or trial-and-error learning.

Instinct means that an animal is born 'hard wired' like the calculator in Chapter 2. The animal responds to a particular stimulus in a pre-determined and inflexible way. For example, the animal smells a certain scent and a set of pre-programmed actions commence over which the animal has no control.

Imitation means learning by copying. Many animals that are taken away from their mothers when they were young are unable to perform certain functions such as hunting or being mothers themselves. This is because many young creatures learn by copying their parents' behaviour.

Trial-and-error learning is the learning by which a rat, for example, learns to run a maze or push a lever to get food. Hoever, a rat that has learned to press a lever to get food cannot 'tell' another rat the secret. Every rat has to work it out afresh. The advantage of language is that it allows animals, in our case human beings, to share their experiences. Hence if any human being learns something such as where to get food or how to make fire, theoretically every human can know the same thing without going through the learning process themselves. What one human knows, all humans can know.

Science-fiction writers have been long fascinated with the idea of advanced beings that all share a common mind. Many futuristic stories tell of super-beings who have a shared consciousness so that if one of them is told something, they will all know. Interestingly, humans have had this power for tens of thousands of years. Through language, humans have the ability to code their own cognitive structures, the elements of their own World Picture, and transmit them to other humans so that a human can not only know everything that's happened in their own life but, *theoretically*, could know everything that's happened in everyone else's lives as well. Of course this cannot happen in practice. No person has time to learn all about every other person in the world.[1] Besides, for reasons that we will see further on, this sharing of cognition tends to be influenced by mechanisms that lock-out or reinterpret enormous quantities of human experience.

Nevertheless, the advent of language created a revolution in evolution. It meant, for the first time, that the learning of each generation could be transmitted to the next gener-ation, which could then add its own experiences to that learning and pass it onto the following one. This is what we call 'progress', which is nothing more than the gradual accumulation of learning from one generation to the next. It is the reason for the dominance of human beings over other biological species on the planet. It is, however, neither as simple nor as beneficial as it first seems.

ORAL TRANSMISSION

As I have outlined, an idea can change its embodiment from a neural configuration in a brain to sound waves to a neural configuration in another brain. Of course we have no guaran-tee that the configuration in the receiving brain will be exactly the same as the one in the transmitting brain. Because people's life experiences are different, their interpretations of words are different and so a perfect replication is unlikely. This leads to a situation where messages can change radically as they pass from person to person. We all know the way that a simple comment can grow into a fully fledged rumour as people pass it around and add their own interpretations and embellishments.

However, we do find that some pieces of oral code re-main remarkably constant despite being retransmitted many thousands of time. This ability of codes to stabilise, despite

---

1   Though the proliferation of afternoon talk shows in the US is taking us
     closer to the possibility.

variations in individual interpretation, allowed the first real doctrines to come into existence.

Prior to the invention of books, few people were literate and written texts were the domain only of specially trained scholars and priests. The propagation of information, news, stories and other ideas was entirely by word of mouth. The transmission of large narrative works was entrusted to professional storytellers. These 'bards', as they were called, were the custodians of the great histories and epics and were required to memorise epic poems of thousands of lines. The division of these long stories into chapters, then into verses and then couplets allowed the professional storyteller to learn the material in chunks. Material such as the plays of Shakespeare were also made easier to memorise by being written in verse.[2] Stories, poems and songs that circulated among the ordinary population also had to be easy to remember if they were going to pass from generation to generation. This is where the idea of *patterns* becomes important.

Take the example of the story 'Goldilocks and the Three Bears'. The story is quite long but is made up of sections that are easy to remember:

- First we establish the three bears: father bear, mother bear and baby bear. This is followed by the set-up of the mother bear making porridge and the bears going for a walk in the woods while the porridge cools.
- Goldilocks enters the house. She tastes the porridge. The father bear's porridge is too hot, the mother's is too cool, the baby bear's is just right, and she eats it all up.
- The situation is then repeated with the chairs: the father bear's is too hard, the mother's too soft, the baby bear's

---

2   Many actors in Shakespeare's time probably could not read and had to have their lines read aloud in order to learn them. In this situation, the rhythm of the lines—as with song lyrics—made memorising the script easier. There was also undoubtedly much improvisation around the roles, hence doubt over the existing texts, many of which may have been written by copyists sitting in the audience and transcribing the play on the fly.

is just right, but she breaks it to bits. We repeat the sequence again with the beds—too hard, too soft, just right. Goldilocks falls asleep.

- The bears come home and go through the whole order *again* as they inspect the damage—'Someone's been eating from my bowl' and so on, culminating in the discovery of Goldilocks in the baby bear's bed.

The thing about 'Goldilocks and the Three Bears' is that all the storyteller has to remember is three types of object: porridge, chairs and bed; three qualities: too much, too little and just right; and two acts: Act 1 where Goldilocks tries out the three sets of objects and Act 2 where the bears return to discover that she has touched their things.

The pattern of the story is so obvious that almost anyone who has heard it can repeat it, even if they have only heard it once. Of course everyone will tell the story in their own way adding embellishments and touches to the various stages. They may even change the wording slightly but the basic elements—the sequence of objects and qualities—will remain the same.

Interestingly, whatever moral or instructional meaning the Goldilocks story might have once had, the principle reason for its being told and retold to this day is that it is a story that almost any parent can remember. One might surmise that its primary value as a story is that it allows parents to impress their children by telling a story from memory.

'Goldilocks and the Three Bears' does not contain the instructions 'Memorise this story and repeat it to your children' but it is the sort of story that will tend to be replicated in any society in which parents tell stories to children because of its ease of recollection. The principle is clear: in any society in which people tell stories from memory, stories that are easy to remember will tend to be repeated more.

Modern-day journalists know that short messages transmit more easily than long ones. People often complain of the modern 'bumper sticker mentality', referring to the form of political debate in which people think and argue in short, simplistic slogans but this has always been the case. From long before the time Aesop wrote his fables, ideas that can be encapsulated in a single sentence have tended to prevail. Consider 'It's no use crying over spilt milk', 'Better safe than sorry' and 'It's an ill wind that blows no one any good'. These proverbs have been the cornerstone of people's thinking for thousands of years. The Old Testament contains a whole Book of Proverbs, albeit expressed in more poetical terms.

The important thing is that proverbs may not be true in any real sense any more than Goldilocks represents a true or meaningful story. The reasons they prevail from generation to generation is that they are easy to remember and will tend to be transmitted more readily than complicated propositions even though the more complicated propositions may be more accurate. Again, it is important to remember that the content of a message may have nothing to do with the likelihood of the message being passed on.

The principle of keeping the story simple (even if the content is complicated) has always been central to doctrines such as religions.

In the New Testament, Jesus (or the authors of the Gospels) uses parables such as 'The Prodigal Son' and 'The Good Samaritan' to communicate complex moral ideas. Rather than simply stating propositions ('We should welcome rather than reject reformed sinners' or 'Goodness is a quality of individuals not ethnic divisions') the parables not only illustrate the principle, they add weight to the idea by giving what appears to be a real-life example. The authors of the Gospels realised a fundamentally important thing: people who have not been formally educated will remember a case study more readily than an abstract proposition, because that is how they have formed their own knowledge of things— through observing events in the world around them.

In regard to the reproduction of doctrines we can therefore formulate a principle:

> 1. When doctrines are transmitted verbally, those with simple easy-to-remember structures are more likely to be transmitted than complicated ones and will be retransmitted with fewer errors.

We can also postulate:

> 2. People whose World Pictures are based on their own experience will be more inclined to believe doctrines that also seem to be derived from personal experiences.

The first doctrines to be communicated in human society were communicated by spoken word. They were the social rules, the stories of creation, the parables, the day-to-day education of the hunting/gathering peoples of the world. These stories and pieces of information were handed down from generation to generation, the more complicated ones often being passed down through lines of trained priests or magic workers who learned their craft through an apprenticeship system.

However, between 5000 and 10 000 years ago, another development occurred in human history, which lifted this process of transmitting cognitive structures from person to person to another level: the invention of writing.

WRITTEN TRANSMISSION

In this book's opening parable, the story of Eve, Eve did not choose to transmit her message by the spoken word. She could conceivably have simply grabbed someone on her way out of the building and said, 'The meeting is on Monday at 9:00 am, pass it on'. Instead she chose to do so by circulating a written memo.

At some point, no later than the time of the agrarian civilisations in the Nile delta and the Tigris valley, people began to write things down. The invention of writing did not immediately have a great impact on day-to-day human communication because most people could not yet read but it did have an impact on knowledge. With the invention of writing human beings became the first creatures on earth to store the contents of their minds externally.

Up till this time, all knowledge, understanding and memory was preserved only in the neural structures of the brain. It could be coded into spoken language but spoken words did not last beyond the moment of speaking. The code could only be preserved, for any appreciable duration, in a human cortex. Writing allowed accounts of human experience to be stored on stone or parchment and, later, to be kept in libraries for all peoples and all subsequent generations to read. Humans thus became the first species on earth to possess an External Memory as well as an internal one. This External Memory had considerable benefits over the internal biological one.

First, it was not limited to a human life span. Prior to writing, no matter how intricate and expansive an individual's World Picture was, it disappeared with the death of the individual. The only way in which a World Picture or any part of it could be preserved was for it to be transmitted verbally to another person, a time-consuming and potentially inaccurate process. Writing allowed individuals to preserve vast slabs of their World Picture in a much more permanent form.

Second, there is no limit to the size of the External Memory. Whereas human beings have a limit to their memory capacity, the External Memory has a potentially infinite capacity. The only limitation it faces is the problem of retrieval. A vast store of information is useless if you cannot find the pieces you want when you want them. For centuries, human society has been dealing with this problem of retrieval by organising retrieval systems such as libraries, the almanac, the encyclopaedia, the Dewey decimal system and, more recently, the Internet.

In the ancient world, societies that created an External Memory had a distinct advantage over others that relied on verbal transmission with its problems of inaccuracy and storage limitations. External Memory allowed people to learn from people who had lived before them, to read historical accounts, philosophical and scientific tracts to which they could, in time, make their own contribution. It enabled a knowledge sharing that vastly accelerated the speed of social development. It also led to a situation where ideas that were written down became the dominant ideas in society.

As psychologist Carl Jung and anthropologist James Frazer have shown, the myths and magic of peoples from around the world have remarkable similarities suggesting common origins or common impulses behind their formulation. Yet each tribe in each region had its own peculiar version of those beliefs, which had been handed down orally from generation to generation.

Those beliefs included creation myths, stories of ancient warriors and kings (heroes or sacred kings), histories of the people and laws for the day-to-day government of the tribe. All of this information was passed on by ceremony, storytelling and tradition, the only concrete aids being some artefacts, cave paintings and icons. However, with the development of civilisation in Europe and Asia, the mythologies of tribes began to be written down.

The impact of writing down a body of ideas such as a religion is dramatic in several ways. First, it allows for much more information to be transmitted in much more detail. Second, it allows for the standardisation of the material across wide areas of time and distance. Third, a religion that is written down will survive when others that exist only in oral form have perished along with their followers. Consider for a moment the fact that the Old Testament, whose earliest stories are at least 5000 years old, is still read and, in some cases, literally believed by millions of people today while the religions of other peoples living in the world at the same time, or even more recently, have been largely forgotten. The Bible is a testament to the power of the written word.

Undoubtedly, had the ancient priests of Judah relied simply on handing down the stories of the Old Testament in an oral form, the religion would probably have been long since eradicated like others from that time. At the very least it would have evolved, changed, or been absorbed into other faiths like the cults of Alcyone, Brigit and countless other religions of the ancient world. Writing down the ancient myths, legends and laws had the effect of slowing down if not virtually halting the evolutionary process that caused those ideas to change slightly from generation to generation and from tribe to tribe. It froze the beliefs in time and created one authoritative version of the culture, which would eventually override all unwritten versions.

It is almost certain that the earliest parts of the Old Testament were originally orally transmitted. Genesis has all the hallmarks of a legend that has been handed down by word of mouth. It has the familiar numerical structure we see in stories such as Goldilocks: On the first day God said, 'Let there be light' . . . on the third day God said, 'Let the dry land appear', each one followed by 'and God saw that it was good' (recalling Goldilock's: 'and it was just right'). Genesis is essentially an easy story to remember, which is why it is probably tens of thousands of years old. The plagues that are visited upon the Egyptians in Exodus, the stories of Daniel in the lion's den and Belshazzar's feast are all memorable tales and undoubtedly come from an oral tradition. However, as one moves through the Old Testament the simple patterns and easy-to-remember dramatic situations become more scarce. The text becomes much more detailed—too detailed for any trained priest or bard to memorise in its totality.

Writing allowed the ancient Hebrews to put together an elaborate and highly detailed set of stories and rules for their religion. It contains not only the creation myths and the hero/sacred king stories (Moses, Samson, David) but a history (though not a reliable one) of the Hebrew people and an incredibly detailed set of laws covering every aspect of Hebrew life from how food is to be prepared and how children should be raised to how marriages are to be conducted and how beasts are to be slaughtered.

It would be safe to say that 4000 years ago every community on Earth had its own myths, social customs, marriage protocols and laws, which probably differed from village to village and region to region but the Hebrew religion is still known today because it had the advantage of being written down. It might even be said that it was the act of writing it down that made it a religion as opposed to simply a set of traditional beliefs. We might define religion as a set of beliefs that have been crystallised into some central, authoritative form.

The importance of having their religion written down was not lost on the authors or transcribers of the Old Testament. The books themselves contain stories that deal precisely with the importance of the *written* word. In the Book of Exodus, Moses goes up onto Mount Sinai where God dictates to him the Ten Commandments and a wealth of other instructions regarding social and religious practices, which Moses dutifully writes down. As if to make doubly sure, God then presents him with a backup copy of the material written on stone tablets. In another version of the tale Moses might have simply come down from the mountain and reported what God had said to him, but the Book of Exodus is stressing how vital it was that a permanent physical record should exist, a text—literally 'written in stone'—backing up the words of the patriarch.

Whether there ever were any stone tablets is unknown but the story in Exodus indicates how central the idea that its tenets be preserved and protected in a written form was to this ancient religion. The whole collection of texts—called the Bible[3]—was regarded as the ultimate authority in the religion, the 'Word of God' no less. Indeed we note that the Jewish religion equates its deity with the idea of words.[4] In contrast with the gods of the pagan world, which existed as mute statues, or animistic spirits of physical entities such as brooks, lakes and mountains, Jehovah was invisible but manifested himself in words. Here was a god who forbade his followers to make images of him and instead manifested himself primarily in the form of instructions coded in language. The Hebrew God is in essence a set of spoken and written tenets.[5]

The issue that concerns us here is the advantage written ideas have over ideas that are simply spoken. From the time of Moses onwards, propositions regarding religion, political theory, history, medicine, geometry and natural history that existed in written form tended to become the accepted authorities. Hence Plato, Thucydides, Hippocrates, Euclid and Aristotle were able to exert enormous influence for thousands of years after their deaths. The Renaissance was a period when the sudden availability of Greek grammar books (because of the invention of printing) enabled scholars to translate and rediscover the historical, mathematical and scientific knowledge of the ancient world. Had these works been permanently lost it is likely that the Enlightenment, which followed the Renaissance, would have been delayed by a couple more centuries.

---

3   Which simply means 'the books' in Greek.
4   By contrast, to the ancient Greeks and the medieval mathematicians
    who revived classical learning, 'God' was to be found through mathematics.
    There was a strong belief among the Christian cosmologers of the 14th
    to 16th centuries (and some mathematicians today) that God is a number.
5   The magic of books and writing pervades much Middle Eastern religion.
    The term 'it is written' still refers to any determination
    of fate or destiny, implying that the entire running of the universe is in
    some sense written in a great book somewhere as in the Persian poet
    Omar Khayyám's poem, 'The moving finger writes . . .', where history is
    allegorised as continuously written text.

This leads us to my next points about the replication of ideas:

3. Ideas that are expressed in written form can contain a far greater amount of information than those expressed orally.

4. Ideas that are expressed in written form change less than those expressed orally.

5. Ideas that are expressed in written form outlast non-written ideas and can be revived even after long periods of inactivity.

This is not to say that written material is not subject to change. In the ancient world many texts had to be translated from language to language and underwent changes in the process. Translators often made mistakes or misunderstood figures of speech and linguistic conventions in the original language. It has been suggested that Cinderella's slipper was originally made of fur but a mistranslation or a mis-copy rendered it as 'glass'. 'Glass' was retained because it added a new level of fantasy and elegance to the scene. Similarly, the idea that Mary gave birth to Jesus in a stable because there was 'no room at the inn' seems to have arisen from a mistranslation of the text. The original Greek of the Gospel according to Luke simply says that the baby was placed in a manger because there was no place to put him in the inn. There is no suggestion that the family was banished to a stable, but merely that the baby was laid to sleep in what was probably a basket. The idea however that there was no room at the inn adds such poignancy to the story that it has become a central feature of the story ever since.

Metaphors and idioms also give rise to problems in translation. Consider for example a modern Chinese translator who was faced with a piece of English text that read

'Janet was on top of the world'. Unless the translator was familiar with modern English figures of speech they might translate this as 'Janet was at the North Pole'. Many ancient texts, particularly religious texts, have come down to us with these sorts of errors in them. Such processes have rendered some passages of these texts quite obscure and yet they are still dutifully studied by scholars. The opacity of the text seems to have added extra layers of wonder and intrigue.

Here I will pause to make another observation:

> 6. A written text possesses considerable authority even if its meaning is not fully decipherable.

Written texts can also be deliberately altered. In the 1st century AD, early Christians produced a large number of religious writings. These included transcriptions of what were originally oral accounts of the birth, life and death of Jesus, letters exchanged by Church leaders and 'inspirational' writings. By 100 AD it was clear that, to maintain theological consistency, the Church needed a *canon*—a single body of officially recognised works. By the middle of the 2nd century the Church settled on the Synoptic Gospels—Matthew, Mark, Luke and John—and some of the letters of the Apostles. Out went Gospels according to Thomas and other works regarded as heretical or politically troublesome. Although it was to be another 200 years before the Church finally agreed on the 27 documents we now call the New Testament, this process of selection produced a set of works which reflected a reasonably, if not totally, consistent account of the lives and teachings of Jesus and the Apostles. Had this culling of texts not occured, the early Church may have fragmented. Thus we might say:

7. Doctrines that demonstrate internal consistency are more likely to be accepted as true.

We also note that written texts, because of their permanency, become an ongoing reference for people's World Pictures. We can express this in the following way:

8. Ideas that exist in a written form can become part of the External Memory and have an ongoing influence on people's World Pictures.

In the 1930s the Nazi party of Germany set about systematically burning the works of Jewish and 'communist' authors—an attempt, unfortunately successful in some cases, to totally eradicate their works. The idea was to remove these texts from the External Memory so that they could not influence individual minds.[6]

This leads us to another point about ideas that exist in a written form: they are more susceptible to centralised control. In the ancient world, the production of written texts was a long and labour-intensive business. Only organisations such as governments and churches had the resources to produce written works and so they largely controlled what was written. With the invention of the printing press and, more recently, spirit duplicators, photocopiers and the Internet, organisational control over the production of written material has

---

6   The notion that ideas contained in books are 'contagious' was not limited to the Nazis. The belief that the External Memory can influence the internal mind is the basis of the efforts to eradicate pornography and other materials that describe violence or sedition. The assumption is that constructs in the reader's mind, and thence their behaviour, will be altered by exposure to these materials.

lessened,[7] although control over the distribution of such materials still tends to be restricted to a few agencies. Almost anyone can write a book, but publishing it requires either a considerable amount of money or the co-operation of a publishing firm.

Methods of transmission that require even more energy, such as magazines, film, radio and television are by necessity controlled by large, well-resourced organisations. Although advances in technology have brought much of this technology within reach of the individual, large organisations still maintain control over the means of distribution. In other words, you might be able to make your own television program using a home-video outfit but you will still require the permission of a television broadcaster to transmit it to a wide audience.

This is illustrated by the fact that libraries, schools and national broadcasting organisations are controlled by governments, commercial broadcasting and publishing is run by increasingly large corporations and a rich nation such as the United States can dominate the television and music industries. From this we might postulate:

> 9. The more energy an organisation has at its disposal the more effective the methods of transmission it can access.

Of course we can also see that the existence of organisations is to some extent *based* on their ability to enable and control the transmission of ideas. This creates a loop whereby, once a country or a company or any social entity

---

7   The anti-war protests of the 1960s, and other student movements of that period can be partially attributed to the invention of the Roneo and the Fordigraph duplicators, which allowed students to cheaply publish their own underground newsletters and communications.

can access a broad transmission base for its doctrines, it will be able to increase its political and economic power, and then increase its transmitting power and so on.

At the same time we see that one of the limitations of written communication and other permanent forms of transmission such as film and videotape is that they require the co-operation of other individuals and groups in society. Speech, on the other hand, remains comparatively 'free'.

EMBODIMENT

Simply expressing an idea in a spoken or written form does not guarantee its survival or its success in competition against other ideas. A self-replicating idea must take steps to see that its code is protected and reproduced. A DNA molecule is a genetic code embodied in a sequence of atomic bonds. By itself it is not effective and is susceptible to decay or destruction by other molecules. So, to preserve and reproduce itself, the DNA builds an extended body—such as a fox—and places copies of itself inside the cells of the fox's body. The fox is then armed with defensive equipment, such as acute hearing and sharp teeth, which enables it to live, fight, mate and pass on the DNA to its young. The fox is a 'survival machine' for the DNA.

Now, consider the instructions in the Book of Exodus for the housing of the tablets of the Ten Commandments and other instructions given to Moses by God.

'And let them make Me a sanctuary, that I may dwell among them.

'According to all that I show you, that is, the pattern of the tabernacle and the pattern of all its furnishing, just so you shall make it.

'And they shall make an ark of acacia wood; two and a half cubits shall be its length, a cubit and a half its width, and a cubit and a half its height.

'And you shall overlay it with pure gold inside and out you shall overlay it, and shall make on it a molding of gold all around.

'You shall cast four rings of gold for it, and put
them on its four corners; two rings shall be on one
side, and two rings on the other side.
'And you shall make poles of acacia wood, and
overlay them with gold.
'You shall put the poles into the rings on the sides
of the ark, that the ark may be carried by them.
'The poles shall be in the rings of the ark; they shall
not be taken from it.
'And you shall put into the ark the Testimony which
I will give you.'

Exodus 25:8–16

These instructions do not specify that they themselves
be included in the ark, but it is implicit that they were. The
important point is that making these elaborate specifications
about how God's rules were to be housed in a special—and
obviously very expensive—box emphasises, in a metaphorical
way, how important it was to preserve the 'DNA' of the religion.

The specific directions about the design of the box—that
it should be clad with gold, which does not tarnish or rust,
and provided with rings and poles so it could be carried
around by this nomadic people—would be the equivalent of
Eve (in Chapter 1) giving the Synaptic employees specific
instructions about how to use the photocopier, what sort of
paper to use and so on. Here, God is leaving nothing to
chance. Thus we might observe:

> 10. The tenets of a self-replicating doctrine must first and
>   foremost include instructions for their own survival.

We can also propose that:

> 11. The more specific and comprehensive the instructions
>   are, the better the chances of survival.

According to Exodus, God then goes on to specify the construction of the tabernacle, essentially a portable church, in which the ark is to be housed. Hence, as the fox stores its DNA within its cells, and the cells are in turn encased within the body of the fox, the law of God is to be housed in an ark and the ark within a temple. Even so, a temple will not guarantee the perpetuation of the religion unless there are people to construct and maintain it. Thus, while the Book of Exodus sets out the rules for constructing the ark and the tabernacle, the Book of Leviticus specifies that the descendants of Levi are to attend the temple and safeguard the ark.

So we see that the body that the instructions create is not just a physical box or a building but also includes a human organisation that will execute the instructions. Most self-replicating ideas systems rely on the creation of both physical and social structures to preserve and spread their teachings. Religions not only organise the building of temples, churches, cathedrals, monasteries, libraries and schools, they also organise the training of priests, priestesses, monks and other devotees who tend the religion and transmit its ideas.

A political movement will usually focus first on human resources with the creation of a political party but, before long, will find it necessary to set up offices and information centres. The minimum embodiment of a doctrine is probably a single academic paper or book. The Extended Body can be a worldwide organisation including such elements as churches, schools, research facilities, universities, industrial complexes, priesthoods, professions, armies, even entire governments that are devoted to the maintenance and spreading of the doctrine.

In the case of socialism, the embodiment of the code is the work of Karl Marx, particularly his *Communist Manifesto* and the book *Das Kapital*. These were published and widely distributed, leading to the code being 'housed' in libraries and universities all over the world. Other socialist texts such as Lenin's *What is to be Done?* contain what amounts to a prescription for organising the process of revolution and the establishment of a communist state. *What is to be Done?* specifies the establishment of committees, working groups, hierarchies, operating procedures and all the other mechanisms required to give the doctrine a fighting chance against its opponents. The Extended Body of Marxism came eventually to include an entire political empire—the Soviet Union and other communist countries—not to mention the existence of Marxist books and supporters in political organisations and educational institutions around the world.

Structures such as schools, libraries, government departments, clubs, armies, books, constitutions, laws and courts have become the standard equipment of civilisation over the last 2000 years. All of them have been constructed by, and exist for the purpose of, preserving and enhancing doctrines.[8] Doctrines may also create uniforms, bodies of literature, songs, poems, medals, statues and ceremonies as further means of proliferating themselves.

> 12. Successful doctrines include instructions for preserving their own code by means of protective structures. These structures will be of both a physical and behavioural nature.

Doctrines do not necessarily have to build such structures from scratch. A doctrine can succeed by taking over an existing organisation. An example of this is the way in which the early Christian Church of Rome was able to use the existing Roman Empire as the foundation for what was to become the Catholic Church. Once Christianity was adopted as the official religion of the Roman Empire after the

---

8   I hasten to point out that 'purpose' here implies no will or intention on the part of the doctrine. It is simply used in the same sense that a fish has fins for the purpose of swimming.

conversion of the Emperor Constantine, the Church organisation was able to use the institutions of that vast political
empire to spread its message across Europe. Although the
Roman Empire had crumbled as an economic and military
force by the 6th century AD, it continues as a *religious*
organisation to the present day. The Christian religion could
never have attained world influence had it not been able to
build on the economic, diplomatic, military and linguistic
infrastructure provided by the Roman Empire.

CHAPTER 4

WHAT'S MY MOTIVATION?

ALL PROGRAMS, BIOLOGICAL, ELECTRONIC or cognitive, are primarily concerned with directing energy. Computer programs do this in a very simple and direct way by throwing switches which send packets of electronic energy along the circuits of a computer chip. The entire function of the computer depends on these packets of energy. Without the flow of electrons the computer is 'dead'—we might say it is not a computer at all, but just a collection of wires and transistors.

The DNA molecule harnesses energy by creating a plant or an animal that acquires energy from various sources, to the DNA's advantage. Plants acquire energy from the atmosphere and the sun. Animals acquire energy primarily by eating.[1] To survive, the DNA must also create structures and behaviours that enable this acquisition. Structures include such things as tentacles, gullets, jaws, stomachs, guts and glands that produce certain digestive substances. They also

---

1   Snakes and other reptiles can also derive solar energy directly by sitting in the sun, which gives them the energy to move around and find something to eat.

include legs for running after food, necks to stretch up to food and hands to grab food. Behaviours include everything from waving tentacles to bring food into the mouth, to hunting, to digging up truffles. All of these structures and behaviours are designed to motivate and facilitate the organism to ingest food and thereby obtain energy. The energy is then used to maintain the organism. Some energy is reinvested in getting more food by hunting or foraging and the rest is expended on survival and reproductive behaviours such as fighting, building nests, mating and child rearing. Ultimately all this behaviour is for the survival and replication of the DNA.

While DNA builds living creatures out of carbon compounds, doctrines build structures on top of the structures that DNA makes. Doctrines exploit the energy systems created by the DNA for their own survival.

So far doctrines have not been able to directly influence the activity of DNA, though they do play a major role in selecting what sorts of DNA are present on the planet. Doctrines have directly or indirectly brought about the extinction, or near extinction of many species on earth and acts of genocide usually represent a deliberate attempt by a doctrine to eradicate a genetic branch from the earth.

A less extreme example of the manipulation of DNA by doctrines is the domestication of animals and plants for agricultural use. As human beings learn more about the functions of DNA we might expect to see doctrines exercising more direct control over biological systems by direct genetic manipulation.

At present, however, the main way in which doctrines exploit human DNA is by influencing *human behaviour*. Ideas can be embodied in written and spoken forms but this does not mean that those ideas will be automatically self-replicating. For replication to occur, the idea must stimulate particular *action* by a human being.

By way of analogy, cold viruses infect the nose and throat causing the patient to sneeze and cough. Sneezing and coughing helps spread the virus to others, and so it multiplies. The symptoms of a cold are not simply by-products of the infection, they are one of the main ways an infection is passed along. Sneezing is a good example of a defence strategy being turned to advantage by an attacker. The sneeze reflex evolved in animals as a means of blasting foreign bodies and irritants out of the nasal passages. However, the reflex eventually became an advantage to the invading organism. By irritating the nose and causing mucous formation, the virus causes humans to sneeze. The virus is projected into space and the infection is spread to someone else. Needless to say, the sneeze only became a reproductive strategy for viruses once people were living, working and travelling very close together (within a sneeze-spray of each other we might say). Hence the development of cities, factories and public transport led to what was a originally a defence becoming a weakness. I will refer to this later on as the Sneeze Syndrome.

HUMAN MOTIVATION

Every action we perform begins as a neural impulse transmitted from the brain to our mouth, our legs, our hands, our facial muscles or whatever part of our body is acting. Before we speak, write, walk, sneer, smile, run, punch, kiss or pull a trigger an electro-chemical signal must be sent from the cortex to the muscle, and that signal begins with a 'go signal' in the brain. No purely cognitive state of the brain (that is to say, a set of cortical connections) can cause a person to act. There must be a firing of a neuron in the *motor* section of the cortex strong enough to trigger the action.

We are familiar with situations where people see an emergency happening in front of them but simply do not move to act. They are typically described as 'frozen' with horror or surprise, but it is usually not so much that fear holds them back as that they simply have no neural connection between what they are seeing and a motor response.

This is often because the situation is so totally new that no connection between the situation and the action has ever been created in their brain. The surprised person has to literally create a stimulus–response connection on the spot, which takes time. The purpose of training—for example, army training—is to give people some pre-existing connections so they don't stop and start forming new brain connections when they find themselves in dire circumstances. The downside of course is that people dealing with emergency situations such as police and military personnel will sometimes not stop to think and do things like open fire on the wrong person.

In so-called lower animals the triggering of action is mostly what we might called 'hard wired'. That is, there are direct links between certain stimuli and certain actions. These are often very simple one-to-one connections. You stimulate a certain part of the creature and its jaws snap like a Venus flytrap. A male moth detects the chemical given off by a female moth and flies towards her. We humans still have many such reflexes in our system. Our pupils contract on exposure to light, our foot kicks if the area below the kneecap is tapped. Our hair follicles erect if we are cold or frightened and we may even fall in love if we detect certain chemicals given off by another person.

In the brains of higher animals, however, the outgoing signal is the result of more than just one incoming signal. It is the result of an interaction between many different neurons that causes a 'go signal' to be transmitted for the physical action. Whether or not a pattern of electrical signals in the brain results in a 'go code' depends on a complex series of multipliers and inhibitors. Multipliers may be regarded as connections that increase the number of signals that converge on the trigger neuron, much like a crowd of people shouting 'Go, go, go!'. Inhibitors are just the opposite. They are signals and chemicals that tend to mute or neutralise the incoming signals, like someone shutting the door so you can't hear the crowd shouting.

We actually experience these processes in our brain as feelings of certainty or doubt. When there is a preponderance of signals impelling us to do a certain action, we simply perceive that action as the obvious thing to do and feel ourselves deciding to do it. If there are signals telling us to do it and not do it simultaneously, we experience a feeling of doubt or hesitation. That feeling of uncertainty is the physical sensation of our neurons and the neurotransmitters in our brains delivering equal amounts of for and against signals. The person may actually verbalise this by saying 'I don't know what to do'. The human may even have to resort to a randomising[2] strategy such as flipping a coin, to break the deadlock.

The firing of our neurons is not only the result of connections between parts of the brain. Behaviour is heavily influenced by a number of powerful chemicals that circulate in the nervous system and affect both the function of the brain and the body's network of nerves. These chemicals are generally known as hormones. Hormones play a vital function in governing the actions of living creatures and are critical to the system by which our actions are determined.

Each hormone prepares the person for, and creates an impulse towards, a certain action. For example, a hungry person might be susceptible to the smell of food and find themselves moving towards the fridge to see what's there. A frightened person will experience a higher heartbeat and their muscles will tense in preparation for fighting or running away. An angry person will also experience a rush of adrenalin and a rising of their blood pressure. Their face may redden and their body may take on a stance designed to frighten others away. A person who is in a state of sexual arousal may also experience increased heartbeat and may start to involuntarily display certain forms of body language. These physical changes are felt by the individual as emotions.

---

2   Randomising strategies are an example of a metarule, a strategy by which we learn to handle our own brain processes.

The person will state that they are feeling hungry, scared, angry or excited. What they are actually experiencing is a chemical preparing their body for, and motivating them towards, some form of action.

What is important about hormones is that they exist in quantitative states.

For example, it seems that during our waking hours a chemical that makes us sleepy is steadily produced in our bodies. After we've been awake for about 16 hours, this chemical makes us want to go to sleep. Sleeping dispels the chemical and so when we wake, ideally, we no longer feel sleepy. The advantage of having a gradually increasing hormone rather than, say, some sort of neural switch is that it can, if necessary, be overridden. Let's say that a hunter has been walking across the African grasslands for 18 hours and is really sleepy. He is just ready to lie down on the ground and shut his eyes when a hungry lion appears. The appearance of the lion produces a rush of the hormone adrenalin, which counteracts the sleep hormone, and the hunter is instantly wide awake and either fights the lion or runs to somewhere safe. Clearly it is important that the need to sleep can be overruled by other needs such as the need to stay alive.

Many other drives, as we call them, can compete with sleepiness, for example, hunger, which can compel us to get out of bed and get a sandwich, maternal feelings, which can drive us to leave a warm bed to tend to a crying child, and sex. A simple reflex mechanism could not accommodate all these competing needs. If people fell asleep immediately when they were tired, the hunter would be killed by the lion, the baby might choke in its cot and human reproduction would be considerably reduced.

So, instead of a set of on/off switches, the human brain has an analog system that quantifies degrees of need by representing them as amounts of hormone—and in some cases, numbers of neural discharges—in the brain. Our bodies are constantly producing different hormones in our brains so at any point we are simultaneously feeling needs for rest, food, excitement, affection, sex and so on. It is essentially the hormones present in the greatest quantities that will rule our neural responses at any given moment. Moreover, there is a hierarchy of needs, defined by the psychologist Abraham Maslow, which determines that certain needs will always take precedence over others. For example, as I suggested before, escaping from a lion will normally take precedence over the desire to sleep. In general terms Maslow's hierarchy of needs starts with the need for immediate physical safety, the need for food, the need for shelter, the need for sex, the need for emotional security—down to the need for self-esteem and 'intellectual' needs such as the need to master one's environment and a need for play. We might surmise that these rules of precedence are an analogy of the strength of the hormones that provoke the drives in question.

What concerns us here is:

- how those controls are modified by the World Picture and
- how doctrines can exploit these mechanisms in order to control behaviour.

EMOTIONS AND THE WORLD PICTURE

Learning is a process of making connections between phenomena, that is to say, all the things we see, hear, feel, touch, smell, taste and experience. Because those phenomena include feelings, the World Picture is not emotionally neutral. It contains important information required to manage the competition between our various needs.

From birth, a child learns to relate elements of the world and their own behaviour to satisfying their needs. For example, toddlers learn to satisfy hunger by reaching out, picking up food and putting it in their mouths. Now move on a few years and consider a hungry child and a freshly baked cake sitting on the kitchen table. If the child were ruled by that learned association in its simple form, they would simply step up to the table and take a piece of cake. The child does not do this however because they know they would 'get into trouble'. The child has a need for food, but also a need for love, and a desire to avoid pain both physical and emotional. No matter how tempting the cake is, the child 'knows', by referring to their World Picture, that taking a piece of cake will result in an angry parent, a temporary loss of affection and probably some other unspecified unpleasantness.

This ability to associate present situations with future consequences is what enables human beings to sacrifice the satisfaction of one need in order to achieve the satisfaction of another. Some people describe this as being able to 'resist temptation' or 'planning for the future' but in mechanical terms it is simply that the emotional attractiveness or fear of the consequences are sufficiently strong at that moment to make it impossible for the person to make any other choice.

A child who is terrified of their parents' disapproval simply cannot reach out for that piece of cake. They may imagine doing it in their heads. They may fantasise about reaching out and taking the slice, they may even be able to actually imagine the taste but their brain simply will not give the command to their arm to reach out and do the action as long as the fear of reprisal outweighs the desire to eat. On the other hand, if something happens that tips the balance of drives, then the child may steal the cake.

UNCONSCIOUS MOTIVATION

Sigmund Freud saw the mind as having three main divisions. The first one was called the id and it was the part of the mind that contained all the basic drives for personal gratification. Freud believed that people are ruled by the Pleasure Principle, which means that they will do what feels good and avoid what does not feel good. All needs—the need for warmth, food, comfort and sex—could be reduced to a basic drive for gratification called the libido. As Freud saw it, a child was born basically all id: simply a small creature demanding that all its needs be met immediately. However, as a child grows, they learn that to achieve their goals, they cannot necessarily strive for them directly. Like the child facing the slice of cake, a child learns that if they want to gratify their needs, they have to learn to obey certain social restrictions, such as waiting until dinner time. This set of rules for behaviour, which moderated the impulses of the id, Freud called the ego.

In our analysis we might regard Freud's concept of the id as equivalent to those built-in hormonal and neuronal mechanisms that create the various drives and emotions. The ego is essentially the World Picture—the brain's map of reality, which includes associations between actions and outcomes. The effect of these associations in the World Picture is to connect actions to gratifications. For example, the child waiting for the cake has replaced what might be regarded as the original association 'taking cake = getting cake', with a more socially aware association 'waiting patiently = getting cake'.

This creation of new associations is what the psychologist Ivan Pavlov called classical conditioning. Pavlov showed that these associations happen quite automatically in a structured environment. Pavlov instituted an experiment with dogs where he rang a bell every time he fed them. Within a very short time he found that the dogs would start to salivate and lick their chops any time they heard the bell. The dogs' physical reaction to food had now been neurally linked to the sound of the bell.

The process of raising children is essentially a process of creating new associations between actions and outcomes. All a baby has to do to gain the parents' attention is to cry. As the baby grows older the parents attempt to broaden its behaviour by making a fuss when the baby does other actions such as talking, walking, building a tower with blocks. They will even reward the child for *not* crying by saying, 'Oh what a good girl, you hurt yourself and you didn't even cry'. Thus, by the time a child is three or four, their World Picture contains a number of associations between behaviours and feelings that tell them that certain actions will lead to the fulfilment of their needs and other won't.

Freud made two more vital contributions to the understanding of these processes. First was the concept of the unconscious mind. As stated earlier, the World Picture includes associations between actions and outcomes, however a person is not necessarily aware of these associations. As Freud showed, a person may be attracted or repelled by certain things without having any idea as to why these things have that effect. They may find themselves performing actions that are to their detriment, but not know why they do them and are unable to stop. What Freud determined was that many of the drive mechanisms and emotional associations that we possess operate without our being aware of them. We experience the result, which may be a fear, a nervous reaction, an attraction, or a reflex action, but we do not experience the reason—that is, the cognitive association—from which the result comes about. This is typical in the case of phobias and addictions and other self-destructive behaviour.

An example of such behaviour might be a woman who constantly forms relationships with physically abusive men, or a man who always seems to sabotage any relationship which is going too well. The person may believe that they have reasons for their actions but the real reasons may reside in certain connections that are operating without their full knowledge. It seems to be that a large portion of our World Picture, some would say the most important part, is not accessible to our consciousness. The Freudian view of the mind was that it is like an iceberg, one-seventh visible above the water, six-sevenths hidden.

The concept of the unconscious mind is closely associated with the second important concept that Freud introduced: the superego. As I said earlier, the ego is the rational part of the mind which allows the person to gratify their id by socially acceptable means. As in the case of the child and the cake, the role of the parents and the parents' affection is central in this process of controlling and modifying the id. Parents use gratification and the withholding of gratification as the principle means of training the child. The parent is established very early in the child's life as the power in charge of gratification.

As a result, associations that parents make between certain actions and certain gratifications become the foundations of the child's behavioural World Picture. The child essentially incorporates the parents' rules into their own World Picture. This means that the child has virtually a *copy* of their parents' World Picture, which exists inside their mind and which continues to act as a parent, even when the real parent is not there. This is referred to by some psychologists as 'internalising the parent'.

Let's return to the example of the hungry child considering the cake on the table. The primary impulse of the child is to reach out and take a piece, but the internalised parent warns the child that to do so will bring about retribution—the disapproval of the parent, anger and possibly punishment. This usually manifests itself as a feeling of fear when the child thinks about taking a piece of cake. The child in the end does not take the cake because the feeling of fear associated with taking a slice outweighs the pleasure at the anticipation of eating it. Even if the desire for the cake wins out, the pleasure of eating the cake is likely to be lessened because of the feeling of fear that will last after the cake has been eaten.

The name we conventionally give to this feeling of fear is *guilt*. Guilt simply means a feeling of fear arising as a result of performing or thinking about performing an action that is associated in our mind with fearful consequences such as feelings of shame. Because it arises from an association that is often unconscious, guilt can arise even when there is no possibility of any actual repercussions. No matter how safe a person may be from detection, the person may have a persistent feeling that 'someone is watching'. In a sense someone is watching and that someone is the 'internalised parent'. No matter how much the person reasons that their actions cannot be detected, in the unconscious mind the action they are considering is still associated with a fear and they continue to receive warning signals from that part of their mind. It is as if a burglar alarm, installed when they were very young, continues to operate despite all attempts in adult life to disconnect it.

The internalised parent, superego or *conscience* as it is commonly called, wields a powerful influence over the behaviour of individuals because it is associated with the strongest fear the child has ever had, the fear of losing the parents' affection. It is also powerful because it is in what we might regard as the 'deepest part' of the World Picture, representing the earliest formed constructs, frequently beyond consciousness and highly resistant to change. Much of the World Picture, particularly the propositions regarding behaviour, will be based on these internalised parental rules.

Doctrines frequently tap into the emotional power of these mechanisms. An analysis of the Old Testament reveals a God who is very like the internalised parent. He is omnipotent—as the parent seems to the child when the child is very young—and holds the power to reward and punish. He is also invisible but at the same time has the power to see everything the individual does—just as the internalised parent has.

It is little wonder that many religions offer a 'oneness with God' as a direct benefit of accepting the faith. It is also little wonder that many people who feel consciously or unconsciously that they are not accepted by others turn to religious groups who assure them that 'God loves them'. The religion offers them the acceptance they cannot find, or do not believe they can find, among ordinary mortals from a supernatural being who, just like the parents of the small child, is always watching over them and loves them.

But religions such as Christianity do not simply wait to encounter individuals who feel inadequate, 'bad' or alienated. The Christian Church has for centuries taught that people are *inherently* bad in the eyes of the supernatural parent. The religion has traditionally taught a doctrine—so named—of original sin, claiming that all people are intrinsically wicked and fall short of the expectations of their 'heavenly father'. The Church offers them redemption and reconciliation with this parent figure through obedience to the Church rules. This doctrine overtly mobilises the energy of millions of people by stirring up, if not actually instilling, unconscious mechanisms.

Doctrines also tap into human emotions through conscious motivations. Through the influence of the parent, the original simple drives of the human being are modified into more complex ones. As the parents attach conditions—such as patience, honesty, self-control, diligence, obedience and kindness—to gratification, the child develops a new range of drives. Feelings such as pride, ambition, competitiveness, frustration and sympathy are essentially transformations of basic human needs which have been given new names by society, just as 'guilt' is applied to feelings of fear of parental retribution. As a child grows up people such as teachers, sports coaches, team leaders, ministers of religion and employers continue the process of conditioning the person's behaviour and beliefs, instilling into the individual what we might call socially modified drive associations.

The effect of these modified drive associations is to teach the individual that to satisfy their drives for food, safety, and so on, they have to perform complex behaviours: go to school, get a job, get a haircut and so on. It is established in the World Picture that there is only one legitimate (that is, approved by the parent) way of achieving satisfaction. Thus the World Picture—our picture of reality—is not merely an intellectual tool but is directly related to achieving those feelings that are sought after by the individual.

13. Doctrines motivate people by appearing to satisfy their emotional and motivational needs.

To appreciate the strength of this connection, imagine a situation where people have a perception that their family, their home, their job or any other aspect of their material wellbeing, is under threat. The threat may be perceived as coming from a political group, a multinational company, a new scientific discovery or an alleged child-molester moving into the neighbourhood; it could be a new fashion in music or clothes or a group of immigrants arriving from another country. Even normally non-aggressive people can become ferocious when trying to protect their territory, livelihood and children. They will mobilise and attempt to defend themselves from the perceived threat. They will denounce the political group, picket the company premises, hurl rocks at the home of the suspected child-abuser and vote against raising immigration quotas.

A doctrine can provoke strong emotions such as these simply by creating the perception of such a threat in a person's World Picture. If a doctrine can alter people's World Pictures in such a way that they feel they have to act in certain ways to gratify their essential needs, then it can effectively control their behaviour. In order for the process to be effective the doctrine must either identify or create a need in the individual and then offer a means of fulfilling that need.

This leads to our next point:

> 14. The emotional or motivational need served by the doctrine can be real or simply perceived.

In summary, self-replicating ideas obtain energy to power their systems by co-opting the energy of human beings. They achieve this by relating the tenets of the doctrine to the fulfilment of basic human emotions and drives that may be conscious or unconscious.

HUMAN NATURE AND INSTINCTS

Much discussion of human behaviour assumes that people are ultimately governed by certain fundamental instincts that are common across the species and will always somehow 'win out in the end'. This is not the case. One of the primary strategies of doctrines is to use human instincts for their own needs. Despite common assumptions about 'human nature', the behaviour of any human is almost totally determined by the doctrines that construct their World Picture. Tyrannical regimes have always known the truth about human beings, which is:

> 15. Human beings can be programmed to believe and do anything.

For example, I postulated above that there is a fundamental human drive among humans to protect their homes and children. But if this is true, how can we explain that for hundreds, perhaps thousands of years, families in certain societies sacrificed their children to gods? Carthaginian couples, 2500 years ago, queued up to place their living babies into a furnace forged in the shape of their god Moloch. Today, young Islamic boys volunteer, and are accepted, as suicide bombers against US military installations while some US parents take pride in the fact that their sons and daughters risk their lives as marines in action around the world. How do doctrines have the power to override the most powerful feeling possessed by humans, the desire to protect their own young?

Once again, the power of doctrine lies in its ability to control the individual's model of reality. If the parent of a child honestly believes that their child will feel no pain in the furnace, or the bomb explosion, but will be transported to a higher plane and live in a paradise among angels they accept the sacrifice of that child. It is not that the parents' protective feelings towards the child are extinguished, they are simply reassigned. Just as the child who has learned not to touch the cake before they are allowed has replaced the proposition 'taking cake = getting cake' with the proposition 'waiting patiently = getting cake', the parents who sacrifice their child in a suicide mission may have replaced the proposition: 'explosives = dead child' with 'explosives = child in paradise'.

Doctrines can also 'bribe' the individual with other feelings to countermand the grief. The US parent of a young marine does not necessarily believe their son or daughter will go to paradise if they die, but they are promised that, should their child die in combat, they (and the deceased child) will receive tremendous honour from their fellow citizens. The notion of dying for your country is elevated to a noble level, accompanied by military funeral and medals, so that while it does not make the loss of a child desirable, or even bearable, it subordinates it to a 'higher cause'. Indeed as we shall see shortly, a doctrine will not be able to survive in a competitive world unless it develops the capacity to override things such as parental protectiveness.

As a result, just as the child's upbringing consists of assigning different behaviours to different gratifications, doctrines can extend that process to reorder the Maslovian hierarchy of needs to place such things as 'the revolution' or 'king and country' and 'preserving democracy' above such things as family loyalties. They do not engender 'inhuman' feelings in the individual but work by connecting human feelings to actions which, seen from other points of view, are detrimental to humans. Thus, during the Cultural Revolution in China children were encouraged to denounce their parents as counter-revolutionary. Such an idea seems unthinkable, and yet, for the sake of 'higher principles' children dutifully sent their parents off to Maoist re-education camps for torture and possible death.

SEX AND MARRIAGE

One instinct that has been substantially drawn upon by doctrines is sex. It is interesting to consider why religions so frequently attempt to prohibit or severely limit the sexual behaviour of people. Part of the answer is that, while the drive for sex is strong, sex is not essential for the survival of the individual so doctrines such as religions can prohibit or limit it without actually harming anyone (other than psychologically). This gives the religion the power to reward individuals for obedience to the faith by allowing them to have sex under specific circumstances, such as a properly sanctified marriage. Thus in the Middle Ages, the Church took control of one of the few pleasures available to the peasantry in pre-industrial society.

The religious control of sex, such as that imposed by the Christian Church, essentially brings the Church into the bedroom. It characterises every sexual act not as an act of the individual, but as a gift from the deity. If a child results from a sexual act the Church can then—quite genuinely— claim to have had a role in the conception of that child. If the Church is to control the shaping of each new generation it must become involved in the training of children even before they are born. The ideal situation for the Church is that each child is born of a marriage consecrated in the Church and immediately baptised into the Church.

The alternative, a society in which people have sex whenever they like, and form short-term or long-term relationships as they choose, essentially deals the Church out of this entire process of bonding and parenting.[3] If the Church loses this power, its role becomes merely a philosophical one. It can preach morality, give advice, answer

---

3   In Nathaniel Hawthorne's novel *The Scarlet Letter* Hester Prynne's
     daughter Pearl, conceived in an adulterous relationship with the local
     pastor, is seen as a beguiling but almost wild little creature. Running free
     in the woods she represents a 19th century fascination with a human being
     who is somehow outside God's realm.

questions of spirituality, provide a focus for the community but it loses its power to withhold and grant pleasure. If people are not dependent on the Church for their sexual gratification, they can choose to abide by the faith or not. Religion becomes optional.

In recent years, the Church has substantially lost its power to withhold and allow sex, just as it has increasingly lost its role as counsellor, psychologist and arbitrator. Church leaders are now working overtime to find ways to keep people in the flock and make the church 'relevant' to society. We might observe that, prior to this century, the Christian Church did not care whether it was 'relevant' or not.

Marriage, however, brings other advantages to the belief system. One possible such advantage to a doctrine is that concentrating a male's genetic 'investment' into a single social unit increases his need to protect that unit. Unlike a man who impregnates many women, the monogamous family man has, as it were, 'all his eggs in one basket'. The theory would be that the man who has one set of children by one mate will fight more ferociously to protect them than one whose offspring are scattered throughout the population. Limiting the fertility of men deprives them of any back-up system in the event that their family is destroyed and enhances the need to preserve the nuclear family and, by extension, the society it is part of.

Marriage however provides even greater advantage to a society when it comes to the vital issue of competition and resource management.

CHAPTER 5

THE POWER TO COMPETE

I HAVE DESCRIBED IN the preceding chapters biological programs such as DNA and intellectual programs such as doctrines create structures and behaviours to harness energy. Of course every doctrine and DNA molecule is in competition with every other doctrine and DNA molecule for those energy resources. The microscopic organism that floats through the ocean, waving its tiny tentacles or flagella to scoop food into its mouth, is itself on the menu for other bigger creatures. One of the richest sources of energy for organisms is other organisms. Even if a creature is not a target for predators, it is still in competition with all the other organisms around it, including organisms with bigger, faster flagella that beat the water more energetically or swim through the water with mouths open, straining the food out with some sort of sieve.

In the case of doctrines I have already discussed how different forms of coding and different forms of embodiment create a survival or a reproductive advantage. We have also seen that doctrines construct social organisations such as churches, clubs and political parties to preserve and promote the tenets of the doctrine. Running protective and reproductive structures such as churches, schools, printing industries and governments requires substantial amounts of energy. In human society energy exists in the form of economic power or wealth; doctrines that can produce greater wealth have an advantage over doctrines which cannot harness similar resources.

To begin with I will consider how a particular set of doctrines made considerable amounts of energy available.

SPECIALISATION

In hunter–gatherer societies most members of the tribe engaged in roughly the same activities—the only differentiation was along sexual lines. Men tended to do more hunting, women gathered food. Both sexes foraged and both sexes engaged in making artefacts and tools. The only specialised person in the hunter–gatherer tribe was possibly the witchdoctor/shaman. At any rate, the ergonomics of hunting–gathering were such that it was pretty much a full-time job for everyone in the tribe, children included, to gather enough food to eat. When the food in any area was used up, or when the game herds migrated with the seasons, the tribe had to move on. All in all it required a substantial investment of energy—walking, digging, running, throwing, wood-carving and stone-chipping—to gain energy in the form of food.

All this was to change with the invention of farming. The domestication of animals—sheep, goats, cattle and pigs—gave tribes access to food in the form of meat and milk, which required a substantially smaller investment of energy. The animals were kept close to hand and the supply was more regular: you could milk a goat every day. The invention of agriculture, the cultivation of crops, produced another efficiency leap. While planting crops required a considerable initial investment of energy in the form of ploughing and sowing, the return in the harvest was a hundredfold. Particularly in the fertile alluvial floodplains of the Nile, the Tigris and the Ganges, a relatively small fraction of the people, farmers, could provide enough food to feed the entire community. This meant that the rest of the community were free to concentrate on practising and developing other specialised skills.

This led to a rapid increase in skills including pottery, woodcraft and barrel-making, and most importantly weapon-making and soldiering. One of the most dramatic effects of agriculture was that it allowed the creation of full-time armies, armies which were going to be needed because agriculture brought with it the necessity to occupy land in perpetuity.

Tribes that were still operating in the hunter–gatherer mode were rapidly vanquished by these energy-intensive societies with their more advanced armies and weapons. The hunter–warrior was no match for the professionally trained, full-time soldier. And herein lies the real secret. It was not just the advent of specialisation in labour per se that conferred an advantage on agrarian societies but the fact that, by specialising, people learned more about their crafts. While the hunter–gatherers simply continued to practise skills that had been handed down for millennia, these new specialists had time to experiment with new and better ways to do things. Trades soon took on their own mystique with each one developing its own system of rank, based, significantly, on skill, its own traditions and its own professional organisation—culminating in the guilds of the Middle Ages.

However, while this new social organisation required less physical energy to be outlaid per unit of energy returned there was a price to be paid and that price was a much more complex system of modified drive associations. Grazing required the ownership of what had formerly been wild animals, available to everyone. Farming required the ownership of what had been public land and tradespeople owned their own materials and tools. The creation of permanent communities (located near farms) required the creation of durable buildings in which people permanently resided. The fact that people now created different types of wealth necessitated the development of some system of exchange, in other words, money.

As a result human beings had to learn some very complicated modifications of their traditional behaviour. In tribal cultures the most serious property offence might have been no more than taking more than your share of the food. In the new 'civilised' society there were personal belongings that had to be protected and so the concept of theft evolved. There were also problems for the less adventurous and the unskilled. The rules of exchange required that if you wanted a share of, say, food, you had to have something to offer in exchange. If you were unskilled, you had a problem. There was no sharing the hunt around the campfire with the whole tribe anymore and there was no digging for yams. The fields were under corn.

Skills in the new specialised trades tended to run in families for the simple reason that, in the absence of technical schools, children learned the skills from their parents. It was thus natural that the children would inherit the tools, mills and farms of their parents in time. From this transmission of skills and land, the idea of material inheritance was born and with it, an even greater emphasis on stable, patrilineal marriage.[1]

RULES RULE

The new doctrines, such as lifelong marriage, which emerged from civilisation were not, however, simply to service the specialised economy. They were socially advantageous in their own right. There has been much discussion in traditional

---

1   Despite the emergence of specialisation, women were still mainly occupied with food preparation and mothering, as they had been in hunter–gatherer society. The newfound skills and the tools, equipment and status that came with them belonged mainly to the men. The passing on of tools and knowledge became a father–son ritual.

social psychology and recent books on Meme Theory about the reasons for the evolution of marriage, monogamy and property ownership. The simple fact is that in a situation where societies are vying against each other for resources, any strategy that frees up energy increases economic wealth, which in turn can make the difference between survival and oblivion. Lifelong marriage is one such strategy. Despite all the conjecture about the way in which marriage assists the raising of children and the preservation of certain genes, the advantage of marriage to a society is that it drastically reduces the amount of time spent on courtship displays, courtship behaviour and fights between rival males (and females).

As anyone who has been a single adult knows, dating is a stressful and time-consuming business. Looking for, choosing and courting a mate requires a considerable investment in time, energy and, frequently, money. Conducting a lifelong series of such relationships would require that sexes devote a considerable amount of time and energy to constantly forming new relationships. It would also entail numerous rivalries and disputes as partners swapped from one to another. The establishment of marriage frees up all that time and energy. If people complain that their spouses aren't as romantic after they're married, it's because that's the arrangement that best serves the prevailing doctrine.

Thus prohibitions against fornication and adultery not only enhance the power of religious doctrine, they provide an economic benefit to the community. A strong family unit that is linked to the church also promotes a uniform morality and uniformity in doctrinal teaching. Societies that have such uniformity in doctrines are also more efficient because less energy is expended by the doctrines in battling each other. In other words, once a set of doctrines—presumably doctrines that co-operate with each other—take control of a society, less human energy is needed for spreading the doctrine within the society and more energy will be available for economic and military developments that will assist the dissemination of the doctrine to other societies.

An example of this is Great Britain in the 19th century—an economically strong nation with a rigid 'Victorian' values that colonised vast areas of the globe and spread Christianity, the English language, British law and a host of other British cultural doctrines abroad. It is significant that the time of the greatest British economic and military expansion was characterised by a period of comparative social stability and a strong work ethic within its own borders. The great economic growth of the United States also occurred in the period after the Civil War when the society took on a substantially unified creed and economic purpose. In both cases uniformity of beliefs promoted, and was in turn promoted by, the spread of universal, compulsory, free education from which, in turn, came greater literacy, technical prowess and economic capacity.

We might note that for many years large corporations have looked closely at their executives' marital situations. Traditionally it was deemed to be essential for a senior executive in a US company to be a happily married man with a wife who was 'socially acceptable'. In hindsight it is easy to dismiss this as a reflection of conservative times and a conservative class of people, however the advantages are clear. The executive in the stable marriage is less likely to be distracted. He is not spending time looking for sexual partners. With a mortgage to pay, appearances to keep up and college education for his kids to worry about, he also has greater motivation to work hard for the firm. Furthermore his preparedness to accept social conventions in his personal life suggest he is likely to adopt the cultural conventions of the corporation.

As far as the corporations are concerned, this sort of selection strategy worked and continues to work. Despite the supposed liberalisation of society over the last 40 years, business organisations still require a substantial sublimation of natural instincts. Concessions in a few areas such as child minding and the (reluctant) tolerance of pregnant executives have been more than offset by greater demands on the individual to be career-minded. Career-mindedness—also known as 'professionalism'—simply means that the person's self-image and self-esteem is based almost entirely on their performance in a business role and their values are virtually identical to the values of the profession or the industry in which they work. We should note in passing that these 'professional' values have nothing to do with directly gratifying the person's needs but are simply ethics that have evolved because they enhance the profitability of organisations.

At the same time, while employers may no longer openly favour the married over the single, the male over the female or the straight over the gay employee, there is greater control than ever of sexual- or courtship-related behaviour in the workplace through the imposition of sexual harassment laws. While the justification for these regulations has always been couched in terms of social justice, there is also an obvious commercial advantage for the employer: sexual displays and rivalries in the workplace consume time and energy in this competitive and globalised world, and that energy is better put into making product and sales.

> 16. Doctrines can increase the energy available for their survival and proliferation by directing the maximum amount of human energy towards wealth creation.

Indeed societies and institutions often benefit from having a pool of people who are not involved in sexual activity at all. From time to time societies have made extensive use of eunuchs (castrated males) in their civil service. The popular belief was that eunuchs were used in the emperor's courts because they were no risk to the bloodline, however eunuchs were also hardworking bureaucrats who were undistracted by wives and children. Western religions have also drawn much energy from the work of monks and nuns.

The Christian Church has for over a thousand years maintained a class of monks and nuns who are sworn to celibacy. This celibacy is often confused with the sexual chastity imposed on Christians as a whole but it exists for a quite different purpose. The rule of celibacy, as outlined earlier, gives the Church the power to permit sex as long as the individual meets certain Church-defined conditions. The celibate devotee, however, is *never* allowed sex, and so cannot be part of this system. The benefit of ecclesiastical celibacy lies in the efficient use of energy.

Doctrines such as religions do not rely on physical reproduction but cognitive reproduction. Thus, while sexual activity is essential to DNA, it can be a serious distraction to a doctrine. Even the most virile man would be hard-pressed to father hundreds of children in his lifetime but a priest who is free of the responsibilities of courtship, marriage and parenthood can be the pastor to many hundreds of parishioners.

From about the 11th century onwards the Catholic Church was adamant that the clergy should be celibate. The intention of this was not just to provide dedicated pastors for local communities but to create a class of scholars who could devote themselves, unencumbered by physical relationships, to reading, learning and intellectually developing the faith. It was this class of celibate scholars who, over the succeeding centuries, formulated, propagated, interpreted and defended the policies and creeds of the church. The rule of celibacy thus recognises that physical reproduction is irrelevant to, and may even be detrimental to, the replication of doctrines. In this sense, celibate priests and nuns are the equivalent of the non-reproducing workers and drones of the ants' nest and the beehive. It is simply better use of energy resources that these individuals not be involved in physical reproduction.

> 17. Doctrines can enhance their strategic effectiveness by diverting the reproductive and nurturing energies of human beings into the strategic development and propagation of the doctrine.

The establishment of private ownership is also a great freer of energy. Disputes over territory or objects are as time consuming and dangerous to a society's efficiency as disputes over sexual partners. Establishing a system of ownership with laws and courts to back it up significantly reduces the amount of fighting between citizens within the society and gives more time for fighting the society nextdoor.

To put it in the simplest tenetic terms, a culture that has rules for marriage, sex and property ownership will tend to prevail over cultures that have no such rules. One of the things that emerges from the study of some impoverished societies is how much time and energy is expended by the members of the culture in non-productive, if not explicitly destructive, disputes with neighbours, rival cultural groups, authority figures and sexual partners. Whole subcultures become locked into a cycle of violence and poverty because their energies are directed in completely non-productive activities.

But wait a minute, you might say. Don't gangsters spend a lot of time shooting each other yet still make a lot of money and resist attempts by law agencies to eradicate them? The answer is yes, but the whole point about organised crime is precisely that it is organised. The history of the Mafia is the history of gangs banding together and imposing rules to reduce violence between gangs for the exact reason that it is was bad for business. These rules are certainly imposed through violence, but their aim is to reduce conflict and maximise (criminal) productivity. It is also worth noting that, as depicted (somewhat too affectionately) in the *God-father* films, the Italian Mafia has traditionally placed great emphasis on the nuclear family and marital stability (though they stopped short of 'marital fidelity'). The dons knew that the breakdown of a boss's marriage was a greater threat to their operation than the FBI.

To reiterate, societies that impose rules to minimise conflicts and competitive behaviours between individuals, such as courtship behaviour and multiple fathering, produce an energy bonus that can be used to strengthen the society economically and militarily. Furthermore, uniformity of culture minimises the amount of energy expended by doctrines in disputes within the society and provides more time and energy to disseminate doctrines to other societies. Conversely, societies that tolerate high levels of interpersonal conflict, mating behaviour and violence may generate successful ideas or practices but they will generally not develop the economic power to spread their doctrines beyond their borders.

It thus comes as no surprise that, after perhaps a 100 000 years of homo sapiens wandering the earth, within a few centuries of the development of agriculture (a blink of an eye in geological time)—civilisations sprang up in Central America, the Mediterranean, North Africa, Arabia and India, creating a girdle of complex, technological, specialised, governed societies around the temperate zones of the earth. If the last three million years (approximately the time since the first identifiable hominids appeared on the earth) were compressed into a one-hour movie, nothing would happen for the first 59 minutes and 52 seconds and then, in the space of about 3 seconds, the ancient civilisations of Sumeria, Assyria, Babylonia and Egypt would suddenly appear. In the remaining 5 seconds empires and civilisations would continue to rise and fall until they covered the entire globe.

CHAPTER 6

THE NOBLE ART

SUCCESSFUL DOCTRINES MUST EMPLOY strategies to deal with other doctrines that may challenge them for control of territory. At this point we should be clear that the territory involved is not a geographical area, though such an area might be involved in the process, but a human mind. The 'goal' of the doctrine is to gain control of as many human minds (and human bodies) as possible. In order to do this a doctrine must eradicate competing doctrines from the mind. There are a number of strategies that a doctrine can employ against the competition.

DOCTRINES OF IDENTITY

If doctrines are to mobilise people against people promoting other doctrines, it is necessary that the people involved know which side they're on. In warfare uniforms and flags developed for this precise reason. Thus, doctrines exploit basic feelings of kinship and familiarity with the surrounding society to create a sense of belonging to a defined group. These programs, which manifest themselves in larger societies, as *patriotism*, *national pride* and even *racial pride* have

89

the effect of activating the people of the society to defend the society (and therefore the program) against other tribes. The more successful the doctrine is at protecting the society or country, the more it will 'itself' survive and prevail.

Identity doctrines typically employ devices such as an extensive mythology that establishes the tribe's pre-eminence in war and culture. They create a strong sense of the moral and intellectual superiority of the host culture and the corresponding inferiority of other cultures. They will characteristically typecast people from other tribes as being dirty, disreputable, untrustworthy, immoral, murderous, ignorant or cursed by God. This kind of propaganda can be found in the Old Testament where the cities of rival civilisations— Sodom and Gomorrah—are depicted as corrupt and amoral and are ultimately destroyed by God for their sinfulness.

These tenets have the effect of justifying aggression and xenophobia against other tribes and cultures, therefore protecting the identity program. (The other tribes of course have their own identity programs as well.) These xenophobic attitudes are marshalled primarily against cultures that present a threat—that is to say, tribes that are in striking distance. Hence tribes will often bear much greater malice to their close neighbours than societies that are far off. As a result the world is dotted with warring pairs of proximate cultures—Israelis and Palestinians, Hutus and Tutsis, Northern Ireland Catholics and Protestants.

THE LOCK-OUT

Let us once more turn to the Old Testament as a model of a highly successful doctrine. Having defined the 'sides' in the dispute, doctrines can now employ mechanisms to discredit the rival point of view. Earlier on we encountered the concept of the 'lock-out'. Consider one of the Ten Commandments: 'Thou shalt have no other gods before me'.

This is recognisable to us from the story of the memos in Chapter 1 as a classic 'lock-out'. It tells the reader to ignore all other religions. It is standard for the tenets of almost any doctrine to denounce all other doctrines whose tenets are contrary to, compete with or question its own. This explains the curious anomaly that religions display more hostility towards other religions and other branches of their own religion than they do towards atheists and agnostics.

The most direct way of discrediting a doctrine is to label it as a deliberate ploy. This usually involves impugning the motives or intelligence of the person who advocates the doctrine. For example, a politician who advocates tax reform may be accused of trying to improve their own financial situation or that of their friends; a person who preaches acceptance of homosexuals may be accused of trying to 'convert' heterosexuals into homosexuals.

The strategy of imputing selfish or destructive motives to people proposing certain ideas works best for small groups and individuals. It is harder to convince people that a whole country is evil or selfish, though it has been done. In regard to ideas that permeate large populations, the principal strategy used by political and religious doctrines is to suggest that the people who espouse rival doctrines have been 'brainwashed'. Proponents of this technique characterise competing thought systems as forms of contagion, while maintaining their own tenets to be scientifically sound. Thus, in the Cold War, the US capitalists spoke of Soviet citizens having been brainwashed by communist propaganda, while the Soviets taught their children that Americans had been deluded by capitalist lies and propaganda.

For centuries the Christian Church has labelled all questioning of dogma as the work of the devil. The invention of the devil as a concept was an invaluable tool for organised religion. Once the idea of an eternal enemy who was intent on instilling doubts in the minds of the faithful was conceived then all dissent could be explained as the influence of the insidious enemy. It was not one's fellow citizens who were evil, but the devil who had subverted their souls and made them act in evil ways. The solution was, all the same,

to burn the citizens at the stake. But this was done as an act
of 'kindness' to 'save their souls', not to silence dissenting
voices or halt challenges to the Church's authority.

This technique, of attributing dissent to some sort of
weakness, provides a plausible explanation as to why there
are other doctrines floating around in society. The same
thing occurs when cultures categorise certain beliefs as madness, ignorance or degeneracy. This is not to say that there
are not mad or ignorant beliefs but just to note that describing competing doctrines as madness or ignorance is a
standard way of discrediting them. To 'discredit' means to
'make unbelievable'. The aim of this is to prevent competing
ideas from influencing people and their behaviour. We can
summarise this as follows:

> 18. Successful doctrines structure the individual's World
> Picture so as to make competing doctrines seem un-
> believable.

PHYSICAL DESTRUCTION

Despite the spread of the Christian Church across Europe,
many ancient myths, beliefs and practices persisted, especially in remote rural communities. These ancient myths
included the continuing worship of animistic 'nature' spirits,
the spirits of the dead, totemistic animal spirits and the
Moon Goddess. Ancient beliefs were practised through
incantations, rituals and the application of herbs. For example, it is believed that many people in remote locations
preserved ancient knowledge regarding birth control and
curing diseases by the use of certain herbs and preparations.

From the 16th century onwards the Christian Church
conducted a ferocious program of eradication of such beliefs.
People practising any form of what were described as 'black
arts' or 'pagan rituals' were denounced as witches and burned

at the stake. These ancient customs and rituals and their preserved knowledge were characterised as the 'work of the devil' and their followers as agents of evil. The religious text *Malleus Maleficarum*, written by two theologians around 1486, spelt out rules for how to identify witches and how to dispose of them. In the 200 years following its publication over half a million suspected witches were executed by the Church.

The attack on suspected witches served many purposes. It seriously depleted the number of people still practising pre-Christian beliefs. It eradicated the knowledge of birth control, which gave women power over their sexual behaviour and lives in general (thus undermining the power of the Church to reward or punish), and it was a convenient way to eliminate anyone who questioned the authority of the Church. Basically, a witch-hunt was an opportunity to denounce anyone that you wanted to remove and have them killed. Thus heretics, political rivals, the insane and any other enemy could be tagged as a witch and burned alive.

The techniques of the witch-hunt provide a pro-forma method for all doctrinal persecutions. Even the term *witch-hunt* has come to mean a prejudicial and vicious extermination of opponents. Opponents are also frequently 'demonised', that is characterised, like the witches, as agents of evil.

Political movements are notorious for this method of combating opponents. Individuals and organisations are depicted as hell-bent on the destruction of the country and malevolent in every conceivable way. Scientists who dared to question the counterproductive agricultural and economic policies of Mao Zedong and Joseph Stalin were accused of being anti-revolutionary, anti-communist subversives out to wreck the party and the country. They were either imprisoned and tortured until they confessed and apologised or were taken out and shot, sometimes both.

Clearly the most effective way to deal with a rival doctrine is to physically destroy its texts and its social structures. In the case of the witches and folk healers, the code, which had been passed down in an oral tradition, was stored in the practitioners' memories—in their brains. The remedy was simply to physically destroy the person, thus destroying the brain that contained the offensive material. The Nazis systematically burned books by Socialist and Jewish writers, seeking to remove all such material from the world. Jewish and Socialist teachers and professors were removed from German universities to prevent verbal transmission of 'corrupting' material to students, and later killed.

In the 1970s, Pol Pot's death squads in Cambodia methodically murdered all educated people in the country in an attempt to eradicate Western knowledge from the country. What is important to note is that, in most of these cases, the aim of these exterminations was to eradicate not just the people themselves but the ideas that existed in their brains. Doctrines may also seek to eliminate brains that stubbornly refuse to be indoctrinated. Thus, the German Nazi party not only sought the destruction of the intellectuals who might challenge their policies, they also executed or at least sterilised, the mentally infirm and retarded.

Imprisoning and killing those who doubt and question benefits the doctrine in that it removes people who might spread their doubts to others. It also creates fear in the minds of other people who might be inclined to question the doctrine. For decades the Soviet secret police ruthlessly rooted out any Soviet citizens who questioned, criticised or satirised any aspect of the communist government. No criticism, regardless of how constructive, was permissible, and the perpetrator would at best be sent to a work camp and at worst executed. The ruthlessness of the secret police and the fact that, being secret, no citizen could tell where they were or whom they were watching (an echo of the internalised parent again) effectively silenced dissent in the USSR for seven decades. Totalitarian organisations are acutely aware of the potential danger that contrary thought systems pose to their power base. This is because, though tyrannies appear to based on force, they are always ultimately based on systems of belief and tyrants know that those who question the truths proclaimed by the doctrine constitute a much greater threat than any armed insurgency.

The physical destruction of the human being is, in all totalitarian regimes, accompanied by the confiscation and destruction of papers and books. Destroying books and other records can be seen as eradicating the External Memory of the doctrine as an adjunct to destroying the Internal Memory of the human being.

The rules in relation to this strategy are:

> 19. Doctrines can hinder the transmission of other competing doctrines by destroying the brains that house them.

and:

> 20. Doctrines can hinder the transmission of other doctrines by destroying any records of them in the External Memory.

MAKING SACRIFICES

A valid question at this time is whether all doctrines must benefit their hosts. DNA as we have seen is a chemical program that builds bodies that will survive, reproduce and thus perpetuate the DNA. It is imperative that the bodies survive long enough to reproduce but once they have done this things are not so simple. Many species are born, grow up, mate, lay eggs and die soon after. Their DNA has programmed them to do this partly because, once the creature has reproduced, it has fulfilled its purpose. There is no genetic advantage in keeping the creature alive. In fact, having creatures live on after they have reproduced can be a hindrance to the next generation because they compete with their own young for food.

In the so-called higher animals, the young need to be nurtured to survive. Human children have traditionally required at least ten years of care from their parents before they have any hope of surviving in the world. As human society becomes more complex that period increases. Children in the industrialised world now require about 18 years of care before they can be left to their own devices. This means that humans, who stay fertile (in the case of the females) until they are in their mid- to late-forties, must live at least another 15 years if their children are to have much of a chance in the world. This sets a minimum age for the death of human females at about 63. Statistics in fact show that 80 per cent of women in Australia live beyond this age.

The reason that humans survive at all after reproduction is because their reproductive strategy involves having a small number of offspring and looking after them intensively to ensure their survival. Other species do it differently. Many simply lay millions of eggs; most of these will die but enough will survive to create another generation of the species. The parents are often as expendable as are the 99.9 per cent of progeny that perish in the first days or months of the birth cycle.

Infectious bacteria also use a variety of reproductive strategies. Clearly, a germ that killed its host before the host could infect anyone else would not be very infectious. If people died before they could pass the disease on, the bacterium or virus would be essentially self-quarantining. It would cause its own extinction. For a disease to be infectious, the victim must remain alive long enough to transmit the disease to at least one other person, or transmit it through bodily wastes or contact with objects. A disease that can hold the body's immune system at bay for a week or so before the symptoms of the disease become obvious has an advantage since the patient may be infectious for some days before they even realise they are sick. The rapid spread of the Human Immunodeficiency Virus (HIV), which causes AIDS, was primarily due to the fact that the virus took years to produce any symptoms. This meant that people simply didn't know that they were infected and continued to transmit the disease to others. The long incubation period was an advantage to HIV. Other viruses and bacteria multiply rapidly and usually achieve transmission very quickly either by breath or physical contact. There is no advantage for these diseases in keeping the human host alive for any significant period so the carrier is allowed to die.

Infectious diseases have become of great concern in the last few decades because of the increased mobility of people around the globe. If everyone on earth stayed locked in their own homes for one year and did not go out, it would be safe to say that a vast proportion of communicable diseases would disappear. Of course this is not possible. Society demands that people move around and meet with each other but it is the prevalence of travel, particularly international travel, that is proving a boon to viruses and bacteria everywhere. Remote communities that were once set in inaccessible jungle are now connected by roads and railways. Airlines now transport people from countries where most people are immune to certain diseases to countries where no such immunity exists.

This is not a totally new phenomenon. The great plagues that ravaged Europe in the 13th and 17th centuries were partly due to the opening up of new sea routes connecting Europe to the Middle East and Far East.[1] Modern travel is a boon to the infectious bug in the same way that sea-travel was and many epidemiologists are 'waiting for the big one' as the saying goes. So what are the implications of social

---

1   Plague spread from rats to humans via fleas. Rat fleas do not normally bite humans but with the death of the rats from plague, the fleas were forced to seek alternative accommodation. Hence the death of one carrier led to the creation of another carrier.

programming? Can the death of the carrier promote the spread of a doctrine?

In ants' nests and beehives the bulk of the worker ants and bees are not directly involved in reproduction—that is, they are sterile. Their sole task is to tend the hive or the nest, which is a support system for the queen bee or queen ant, the real reproductive unit. The worker ants and bees are completely expendable. Their job is to build the nest, gather food, tend the young, tend the queen and, if necessary, die in the defence of the nest. Bees, as we all know, die after stinging yet bees will all attack and sting an animal that threatens the hive.

The worker ants and bees all grow from eggs laid by the queen. It is the ferocity of their attack and their willingness to sacrifice themselves in the defence of the colony that ensures her survival, and the transmission of the DNA to the next queen. In this case the structure that the DNA builds is not just the insect itself but the whole nest. Bee hives, and ants' and termites' nests should be regarded as organisms in their own right.

Obviously this capacity for self-sacrifice by selected members of a community occurs in human society as well. For thousands of years there have been people whose job is to defend the rest of the group and, if necessary, die in the attempt. For centuries, dying for your country was regarded, and still is by many people, as the most noble act a citizen could perform. The cities of the world contain thousands of monuments and statues commemorating people who 'laid down their lives for their country'. Many fanatical political and religious groups have members who are prepared to 'die for the cause', giving rise to suicide bombers and so on.

The important thing is that this behaviour is not, like the bees' or the ants', programmed by the DNA. The human warriors who marched off to die in wars for the last 10 000 years were not sterile, nor were they born purely for that purpose. The sacrificial role was imposed on them by cognitive programs not chemical programs, but the strategy was the same. The society that organises a squad of strong aggressive members to defend the community is more likely to survive. If those defenders feel (note the importance of feelings) strongly enough about what they do to die defending the community, that's all the better.

If the warriors are prepared to risk death not just in defending the tribe but attacking other tribes as well, better still. This means that the community is well placed, not only to protect itself, but to attack, destroy or subjugate other communities and thereby gain a greater share of those all important energy resources.

Thus, in line with the strategies of DNA and micro-organisms, we can say the following:

> 21. If the propagation of a doctrine is assisted by the death of the human host then the host will be killed.

CHAPTER 7

SPREADING THE WORD

UNLIKE ANIMALS, DOCTRINES DO not need to 'mate' to reproduce, though, as we will see later, they are subject to their own version of recombination. Doctrines reproduce by copying themselves, like Eve's memos, from brain to brain. In societies where doctrines are established, this occurs when parents and teachers educate the children of each generation. But how do doctrines spread into new areas?

EVANGELISM

The simplest technique a doctrine can employ is to send out emissaries, like a chain letter, to spread the doctrine as far and wide as possible. We can postulate that an evangelical religion that dispatches missionaries to every part of the world will build its numbers much faster than a religion that waits for converts to come to it. Similarly a political movement that establishes chapters in many cities and actively recruits members will rapidly overtake an organisation that operates out of a small office and hopes people will be converted to the cause.

The New Testament, which is the basic instruction book for the Christian religion, tells, in the Acts of the Apostles, the story of the disciples, soon after the crucifixion, being given the power to understand the languages of all the people in Jerusalem. This story was a way of indicating to the early Christians that they were to travel across the world and spread the teachings of the Gospel. This is probably the first recorded account of a missionary approach to religion and it has remained an effective technique of gaining new converts for 2000 years.

MIMICKING STRATEGIES

We know that many living creatures protect and gain advantages for themselves by adopting the colouring or features of other creatures or objects. The most obvious is camouflage where the creature conceals its whereabouts by being the same colour and patterns as its surroundings. Some moths frighten away predators by sporting a pair of staring eyes on the backs of their wings. Some species of frog are the same colour as poisonous species although they are not themselves poisonous.

Belief systems also can establish a foothold in the human mind by looking like something else. Like the harmless moth that sports the eyes of a predator, doctrines can adopt the 'look and feel' of things that are quite the opposite of what they are. Examples of this would be extremist militia movements that advocate armed resistance against the government describing themselves as 'patriots', or Christians who call themselves Christian Scientists while opposing scientifically validated medical treatments. Totalitarian movements will often describe themselves as liberation armies, or freedom fighters.

Opponents of such movements tend to imagine that they adopt these names, the opposite of what they really are, as a deliberate ploy. The truth is that most people belonging to these movements really believe that they *are* patriots, scientists and liberators. The doctrine has reprogrammed their definitions so that, for example, a revolutionary army can, with a clear conscience, impose dictatorship on a country in the name of 'freedom'.

I will explore the manipulation of definitions later. For now, let us simply say that it is easier for a doctrine to infiltrate a population if it in someway resembles belief systems that are already resident in the world pictures of the people. For example, a person may resist the idea of committing murder because the belief system in which they have been raised forbids it. The idea of killing someone causes feelings of guilt and anxiety to emanate from the internalised parent or superego. However, if killing can somehow be made to look like a virtue, the individual may be swayed towards the idea. A radical movement has only to convince someone that certain people such as politicians, intellectuals, millionaires or a particular ethnic group are actively harming the community, and the idea of killing may take on the semblance of a good thing. Hence militant left-wing revolutionaries can contemplate the killing of powerful business people without guilt and extreme right-wing militia groups can express pride at bomb attacks on government buildings, even regarding the collateral death of children as a 'regrettable necessity'.

Terrorist and other extremist organisations undoubtedly recruit members who have high levels of aggression, and they utilise that aggression by creating an association between violence and morality. It is the fact that there is a pre-existing sense of morality in the society that allows the doctrine to manipulate large numbers of people towards violent acts. A society of people who were largely amoral and cared only about themselves might easily be persuaded to commit violent acts for personal gain, but it would be hard to forge them into a society of zealots. It is difficult to motivate a totally selfish person to commit acts of violence that involve no profit to themselves, but a person with a highly developed sense of justice can be persuaded that extreme measures are necessary to overthrow an evil regime or stop an immoral practice. Thus, paradoxically, intelligent and even sensitive individuals, who would describe themselves as being fundamentally moral, can end up bombing a crowded railway station to protest about foreign rule of their country or shooting a doctor who works at an abortion clinic.

This is not to say that non-violent people are the most likely to turn violent but that, rather than being safeguards against violence and oppression, inculcated notions of morality or justice can become the very tools that doctrines use to justify what we would otherwise regard as immoral and unjust acts.

In fact very few doctrines propagate by challenging the pre-existing belief systems of the society. Rather, they go to great lengths to appear to be reinforcing those beliefs. Many movements, even though they propose new and radical changes, represent themselves as being 'back to basics' or 'a return to fundamental principles', 'getting back to old fashioned values' or 'standing for law and order' and so on.[1] Such appeals are very persuasive because they draw on some of the first-learned, and therefore most strongly felt, principles in the human mind. The ideas of reward and punishment and parental authority are among the first notions to be instilled in the child and form some of the most universal notions in civilised society. When political movements call for a return to moral principles they are enticing people to return to the state of certainty that they experienced as children. Those movements seek to capitalise on the strong bond between child and parent and essentially promise to reinstate the conditions of childhood where goodness is rewarded and badness is punished. These ideas are of course expressed in adult terms—for example, 'people who work

---

1   For example, pro-gun Americans will argue for the right to own and carry high-powered machine guns by referring to an Amendment of the US Constitution passed in 1778 that was intended to apply to swords and muskets.

hard should be rewarded by tax breaks', 'people should not be paid not to work' or 'people who commit murder should be hanged'—but they still essentially reflect the moral structure of a child's world. Doctrines may even set out to discredit anything that conflicts with that childish view, denouncing specialised knowledge or science as being 'elitist', or 'left-wing' or even 'the devil's work'. These tactics basically tell the individual that life can be as simple as was when they were five years old; the doctrine then moves in and stands in loco parentis—in the place of the parent.

Each successful doctrine, therefore, be it religion, political movement or management theory, in some way builds on and reflects the family structures and the traditional values of the society that it colonises. Societies that have strong father figures will tend to support churches with patriarchs and political systems with kings. They may also generate intellectual subcultures that are radical and revolutionary but still dominated by strong male leaders.

The Christian missionaries who introduced their faith to Rome found it necessary to slightly alter the focus of their religion. In Judea, Christianity was, like its parent religion, based on a male god with the addition, in Christianity's case, of another male figure—his son. The Romans, with their long history of worshipping many gods and goddesses including Venus, Minerva, Juno, Diana and, in the 2nd and 3rd centuries AD, Isis, tended to demand a goddess of equal importance. This created a problem since there were no female deities in the Jewish faith. Jehovah was a bachelor. To solve the dilemma, the Roman branch of the Church dramatically increased the importance of Jesus' mother Mary, who was a minor figure in the Judean faith, so as to make her a major feature of the cult. The result was that Romans who had formerly worshipped Diana (a virgin goddess), Venus (a goddess who was capable of renewing her virginity) and Juno (the mother of the gods), switched to worshipping Mary, a figure who combined elements of all three. The cult of Mary became, and remains to this day, a central part of Roman Christianity.[2]

This process continued as the Christian Church spread across Europe. As it reached new lands, the faith changed to incorporate existing regional religions and traditions. Local pagan gods—such as Brigit, the British Moon Goddess—were recreated as saints. Christian significance was added to ancient ceremonies. The northern midwinter 'yuletide' festival was declared to be Christ's birthday and thereafter celebrated with a mixture of symbols: the star, the stable, the manger, the shepherds and the three kings coming from eastern Mediterranean mythology, the Christmas tree, the holly, the mistletoe and feasting coming from the original Teutonic festival.

Similarly the European spring festival, when people celebrated the rebirth of the land after the winter, was converted into a celebration of the death and resurrection of Jesus. Symbols of the crucifixion thus ended up being mingled with pagan symbols of fertility—the rabbit and the egg. Although most people cannot see any connection between these ideas today, in 7th century Europe there was an obvious connection between the resurrection of the earth after the 'death' of winter and the resurrection of the sacred king.[3]

Political analysts are quick to point out that communism as practised in China is quite different from communism as it was practised in the Soviet Union. The reason for this is not just that the Chinese set out to adapt communism to their country but simply that only certain forms of communism

---

2   A myth was devised that, after the resurrection, Mary's house was lifted by angels and carried to Rome where she lived out the rest ofher life. Thus, though Roman Christians could not confer Roman citizenship on Jesus, they could do so in regard to his mother.

3   In neolithic Europe, 'sacred kings' were sacrificed (often by being nailed to trees) to ensure that the earth would awaken from the snows of winters. The story of the crucifixion appears to be directly related to this idea— the King of Heaven dies in order that everyone else may experience renewal and rebirth. Today this is taken to be a spiritual rebirth but to the early Europeans it was primarily an environmental resurrection: the rebirth of the soil for the planting of the crops.

could gain acceptance in the Chinese social environment. Like a new species entering an environment, some variations of a doctrine will survive better than others. As we will see later, systems of thought are constantly producing such variations and some variations will survive and proliferate in some environments better than others. From the time of its formulation Marxism has continued to diversify into different versions, one version taking hold in Russia, another in China. Different versions again have taken hold at various times in Cuba, Chile, Nicaragua, Ethiopia, Vietnam, Cambodia and Yugoslavia. Each one of those strains emerged because it was in some way suited to the social conditions of that country.

PIGGY-BACK STRATEGIES

Biological science recognises three types of reproduction. Sexual reproduction where two DNA molecules combine to form a new organism, the direct splitting of a cell into two identical cells such as occurs with bacteria, and reproduction by inserting DNA into the DNA of another organism—the strategy used by viruses.

Viruses are little more than small packets of DNA that invade the cells of an organism and splice themselves into the DNA molecules of those cells. When the cell duplicates its DNA and then divides into two new cells it automatically copies these blocks of viral DNA as well. At a later time, the newly duplicated viral DNA blocks create copies of themselves in the cell, which break out through the cell walls, killing the cell, and go looking for another cell to invade. Thus the virus, which has no capacity to reproduce by itself, uses the cell's reproductive mechanism to duplicate itself.

Thought systems can also reproduce by attaching themselves to existing self-replicating structures. People involved in running churches, political parties and other committee-based organisations will be familiar with the phenomenon of 'factions' or 'pressure groups' trying to swing the policy of the organisation in a particular direction. Existing office bearers will often complain of people trying to 'hijack' the organisation.

It is always a matter of concern for the custodians of social institutions when they see the growth of divergent policies within their organisation, since there is a threat that these policies might take over and start to steer the organisation as a whole. Examples of this are the growth of a communist wing in a labour or social reform party, the formation of an ultra-right-wing in a conservative party or the emergence of a liberal movement within a church. Setting up an entire movement with all the resources and political contacts required can be a daunting task. A much more efficient strategy is to infiltrate an existing influential organisation and alter its policies and activities in the desired direction.

The doctrine of Marxism was particularly successful in copying itself into certain institutions. These included, naturally enough, trade unions but also, less obviously, educational institutions. The doctrine did not, initially, have the power or the resources to set up its own independent schools and universities, as churches have done, but it was able to penetrate the existing academic system. This was made possible partly by the nature of the doctrine itself.

Because it was embodied in *Das Kapital*, a huge tome of economic and historical theory Marxism appealed to academics. Like medieval Christianity, the doctrine was too complex for the layperson to understand, thus ensuring that people would require an elite class of priests (academics) to interpret it for them.[4] Like Christianity, it also offered a theory of society and history that could be used to interpret

---

4   Capitalism on the other hand is basically easy to understand. Despite the attempts by economists to create sophisticated economic schools of thought—'Galbraithian' and 'Keynsian' economics—capitalism requires few priests to interpret it and is passed on by practitioners or simply learned by imitation. The fine points of the system are analysed, developed and applied by accountants, bankers and financiers who are essentially craftspeople rather than theoreticians.

almost any phenomenon. This enabled academics, throughout the 20th century, to produce theories, papers and courses based on Marxist interpretations of art, literature, science, culture, sexual behaviour, morality, foreign policy and history—virtually every field of academic discourse.

> **22.** Doctrines can spread through a population by exploiting the structures and tenets of existing doctrines.

NURTURING AND MAINTENANCE

To survive over a long period, a doctrine must not only access a supply of energy in a population, it must set up a system of maintenance to ensure that it maintains its control over that energy supply. Consider the Hebrew invention of the Sabbath, a particularly brilliant innovation. The rules of the religion set aside one day out of seven for consideration of the faith itself. First, this rewards the faithful by allowing them to do no work for one day each week—a radical concept in an age when people worked every day from dawn to dusk—and does so without seeming to promote laziness by declaring the day to be a day of worship and consideration of higher things. Most importantly it connects the religion to the community's time cycle, making time itself a religious concept.

Most religions prior to Judaism celebrated specific days of the year such as the midsummer and midwinter solstices, the nights of the full moon and the annual flooding of rivers. Judaism may be the first religion to have created a religious holiday every seven days.

The Ten Commandments also decree that one should honour thy mother and father—an important tenet. This, first of all, reinforces respect for the parent. Since the Jewish God is a parental figure, enhancing respect for the parents also enhances respect for God. More importantly it is a direct incentive for the parents to instil the commandments in their children. Ask yourself, how many parents would raise their children in a religion that taught them to disobey their parents. If they did, the whole religion would die out in one generation.[5]

SHELL STRATEGIES

Self-replicating systems do not have to multiply to survive. Some strategies are focussed on preserving a small unit of the doctrine over a long period of time. The creation of a priest class provides such long-term protection for the tenets of a faith. Just as a tortoise protects its body with a hard casing, some doctrines encase themselves in secrecy and elaborate recruitment rituals.

In the ancient world, both religions and mystical scientific sects such as the Pythagoreans shrouded their teachings and their organisation in secrecy. Rather than relying on an aggressive recruiting strategy, these systems actually made it very hard for the individual to join the cult or sect. This ensured that by the time the proselyte had undergone all the training and passed all the initiation tests, they were well and truly steeped in the beliefs of the organisation. This minimised the likelihood that, once they were accepted into the inner sanctum, they would start to challenge the fundamental tenets of the system.

According to this strategy, those who are inducted into the group are charged with protecting the beliefs and ensuring their continuing survival over the centuries. They are regarded as the 'keepers of the flame' and entrusted with

---

5   Note that in the Cultural Revolution, young people were encouraged to disobey and even denounce their parents if they saw them acting as 'bourgeois reactionaries'. This is because Maoism—a first-generation doctrine—did not rely on parents for its transmission to the younger generation. The tenets of Maoism were spread by youth organisations, posters and the notorious *Little Red Book*. Modern communications also have the power to subvert parental teaching, and frequently do as I noted in Chapter 2.

many secret rules, documents and sacred objects. It is their responsibility to see that the beliefs, the 'knowledge' and the moral code of the society are passed on from generation to generation. Of course, to make sure they do this, there has to be a training and selection procedure that ensures that those who are entrusted are absolutely reliable, in other words, fully indoctrinated and not likely to suddenly decide that the whole thing is a waste of time and terminate the whole process.

The secrecy surrounding the beliefs prevents others, who have not been fully indoctrinated, from raising questions about them—that is to say, secrecy protects the system from other belief systems which might destroy or pollute it. Such strategies have been used to maintain secret knowledge in tribal societies for thousands of years and account for the continuation of societies such as the Freemasons and the Rosicrucians.

> 23. Doctrines can protect and preserve their code by placing it under the care of specially selected and indoctrinated individuals.

To summarise what has been discussed so far, doctrines spread through human societies by employing survival and reproductive strategies in the same way that DNA configurations manipulate biological systems to reproduce. Whereas DNA had adapted to its environment—that is, the surface of the planet earth—and created animals and plants that can compete for survival in that terrain, doctrines have adapted to their environment—that is, human society and the human brain. They have 'learned' through selection how to derive energy by manipulating human emotions and drives, how to organise human society to reproduce themselves and compete with other doctrines and how to store themselves in 'hard copy' form in external locations.

Like biological systems, doctrines do not rely on one particular set of strategies but rather, as animals employ shells, horns, speed, camouflage and a variety of different reproductive and hunting strategies, they employ a wide range of tactics to enable them to colonise human beings and multiply.

Like biological systems again they work in conjunction with each other, feeding off each other, using fragments of each other to enhance their own position and, when necessary, destroying rivals. In doing so, like biological systems, they have altered the terrain in which they live. As animals will coexist with some species and ferociously attack others, they have selected some human beings for survival and eradicated others.

So just as in an earlier stage of the earth's history, amino acids joined together to make self-replicating molecules that populated the planet with plants, animals and bacteria, over the centuries, propositions grouped together to form doctrines—integrated systems of propositions—which in time covered the earth with cities, nations, religions, cultures, sciences and so on. From the moment that humans developed symbolic propositional language the evolution of these doctrines became the most significant process on the planet, overtaking the evolution of DNA as the primary shaping influence on earth.

In fact, the modern world is almost entirely the result of the operation of doctrines. Doctrines build armies, cities, schools, libraries, ports and farms. They create and enforce laws, institute social programs, run economic systems, create arts and entertainment. All the things that humans take credit (and blame) for in the evolution of civilisation across the earth are the results of competition between doctrines— the dominant form of self-replicating systems on earth.

CHAPTER 8

THE EVOLUTION OF IDEAS

So far I have been discussing the ways in which doctrines compete with each other for dominance of a territory. The question is, where do doctrines come from in the first place? How are new doctrines created? Traditional thinking holds that ideas are created by human beings, that individual human minds discover or invent ideas that are then adopted by others. This is the cognitive equivalent of Creationism in the physical and biological sciences. What I will propose here is that the designs of doctrines have not come about intentionally. Ideas evolve in the same way as the DNA molecule has evolved.

Biological programs such as DNA were never written by anyone but have resulted from gradual evolution over billions of years. That evolution has come about because of the existence of two factors, which are the basic requirements for any evolving system:

1. Variation: there must be different versions of the self-replicating system that perform differently in the environment.

2. Selection: some process in the environment must remove some of the variations, leaving others that go on to reproduce.

If DNA were a perfect replicator, life on earth as we know it would probably not have evolved. Evolution has only been possible because biological reproduction systems make mistakes. Errors in replication result in differences between offspring and their parents. Usually the errors—or mutations as they are sometimes known—are useless and either disable the creature or have no effect on its survival potential. From time to time, however, a variation occurs that gives the individual an advantage over its peers. That creature will then survive and pass its unique characteristic on to its descendants.

A system of reproduction that always resulted in perfect copies would halt evolution because no new features would ever appear. Conversely, a system that was too inaccurate would lead to the rapid extinction of the entire species because essential features such as stomachs, eyes and brains would be missing too often. Thus a system that allows evolution will be a system that causes errors occasionally, but not too often. Even so, DNA mutations tend to involve dramatic changes in the organism, such as the addition or removal of whole limbs, and beneficial changes do not occur frequently enough to allow the species to adapt to shorter term changes in the surrounding environment. Luckily there is another system that is able to fill in the gaps.

Sexual reproduction is a system that manages to allow the reproduction of all the beneficial features of the organism with a high degree of accuracy but with some degree of variation from which new features can emerge. It involves two individuals combining their DNA to produce a new being. The basis of sexual reproduction is the mixing of two sets of genes that produces offspring similar to, but not clones of, their parents. The combination of DNA from two parents provides a range of variation, without relying on mutation, from which individuals best suited to their environment can be selected while the occurrence of dysfunction is minimised.

Take, for example, an ancestor of the camel, a small deer-like animal living in semi-arid regions. Two such creatures mate and produce six or seven offspring. All the offspring possess the physical characteristics of their parents, including an ability to store water in their fat cells but, because of the way sexual reproduction works, they will vary in this capacity—just as all brothers and sisters vary in height, weight, colouring and so on. Let's imagine that one or two of the offspring have a greater tendency to retain fluid than the others. Now imagine that the area goes through a climatic change and starts to become drier. Droughts occur. The young pre-camels who are better at retaining water survive the droughts better than their siblings. They meet and mate with pre-camels from other families who—if they have survived the drought—probably share the same water-retaining abilities. The result is a new generation of creatures who have a higher rate of water-retention than their grand-parents. But even among this new generation there will be variations. If drought comes again, once more the ones who retain the most water will tend to be the survivors and the ones who are more likely to reproduce. After a few hundred generations of this process the result will be a species of animal that has a considerable water-retaining ability—in other words, the modern camel.

The development of a characteristic such as the ability to retain water does not necessarily require the mutation of genes. It simply requires a change in the concentration of certain gene combinations in a population. A particular environment will favour certain genetic combinations over others.

So far I have discussed the ways in which doctrines compete with each other and how the successful doctrines are those that have efficient or permanent forms of coding and manipulate human beings in such a way as to cause them to create structures and perform behaviours that will result in the survival and replication of the doctrine. In other words, I've been outlining the process of selection. But what of variation? How do different doctrines or variations on doctrines arise in the first place? Trying to apply the idea of variation or mutation to learning by imitation or trial-and-error doesn't make much sense but it is easy to see how these things can occur with ideas that are transmitted by language.

MUTATION

I have already mentioned that errors frequently occur in the transmission of doctrines and we have also seen how those errors can become permanent amendments to the doctrine—such as Cinderella's glass slipper and the story of Mary and Joseph being turned away from the inn. Sometimes the acceptance occurs because the error accidentally creates a new tenet that appeals to people; for example, the pathos of the pregnant virgin being sent to the stable. However, appeal is not absolutely necessary. Sometimes an error will be simply accepted and reiterated because of the authority of the doctrine that it is associated with.

Strangely enough one of the mechanisms that causes errors is one of the most vital functions of the human brain: generalisation. Humans are constantly receiving sensory input from their perceptual system engaging in mental activities and experiencing emotions. These sensations are not only experienced at the time, they are recorded as memories so they can be re-experienced again later. Memories are not stored in random or chronological order, nor in isolation from each other, but connected in such a way as to reflect the real world. In the brains of Pavlov's dogs, for example, memories of the taste of food, the sight of food, the smell or food and the pleasure of eating food are connected to the memory of the sound of a bell. The sound of the bell becomes associated with the experience of eating food. These stored memories become connected and differentiated so to create in the brain a set of neural associations that correlate structurally with the outside world. Things that are associated with each other in the real world are, ideally, associated with each other in our brains. This is what we mean when we say that our World Picture is a 'map' of our environment.

The problem with building a mental map of the universe is of course that we can only see a small part of the universe at any one time. The entire cosmos is never revealed to us but rather we have to build up our model of reality bit-by-bit as we go along, like a surveyor painstakingly making their way along a coastline. Each new experience adds a bit more information to the map so it becomes more and more accurate, but at any given time our concept of reality—what we hold to be true—is derived from the total of what we know at that point. In other words, our general rules are based on our specific experiences. This process of generalising—or deriving general rules from specific instances—is what scientists call 'induction' and it is the basis of most of our science. We observe phenomena and from them we formulate hypotheses about the nature of the world.

However, the process of induction is not the result of a higher order mentality but an automatic cognitive operation that occurs in most animal brains. It is demonstrated by Pavlov's dogs who salivate at the sound of the bell because they have induced a general (though non-verbal) concept that 'bells mean food'.

An inability to form generalisations would constitute a severe learning difficulty. A creature unable to form associations from its experience could not apply learning from one situation to another and would live in a world that constantly seemed new and surprising. It would be constantly stumped as to what do. In reality, however, after having tipped over one garbage can and found something to eat, a dog rapidly learns to associate all garbage cans with food. A rat that learns to push a lever to get food in one cage will quickly perform the same actions if presented with a similar lever in another cage. A child will be eager to go to Grandma's if they remember getting a lolly last time because they will expect to get one again.

Generalisations can lead to errors, however. Pavlov's dogs will salivate even if the bell is rung accidentally. A dog who has been beaten by its owner will run away from anyone, even if they are someone who is kind to dogs. What this indicates is that generalising is not something that has to be learned. It is hard wired. What has to be learned is *not* to generalise.

In the history of human society many doctrines have come about through incorrect generalisation. Ancient humans sought to explain the natural world phenomena by generalising from what they already knew. They observed large rocks lying on the plain, miles from the mountains. Today we know they were left there by glaciers in the ice age but ancient people had no way of knowing that. They generalised from what they knew. Humans threw rocks around so it was reasonable that the rocks on the plain must have been thrown there by giants. People were aware of the fact that animals such as dogs and birds came in different sizes so it was quite plausible that there may be, or may once have been, very large humans.

Clouds, stars and tides moved and changed, and again it seemed logical that powerful beings, magical human or animals, must be the cause of these events. A whole range of anthropomorphic myths evolved: magical super-beings who, though they were more powerful, had wars and love affairs and children, just like humans.

Nor were these types of extrapolations confined to the hunter–gatherers of the world. Right up until the 20th century eminent philosophers and scientists argued that because the world shows evidence of order, it must have been designed by an intelligent (human-like) creature. The reasoning was simple. The visible universe with its planets and stars and moons operates like an intricately tuned machine. Human beings design and construct intricate machines, such as watches, so the universe must have been constructed by some sort of super-intelligent human being. This argument for the existence of an intelligent God, the great designer, has been regarded for centuries as irrefutable logic and yet it is no more than a crude extrapolation from one idea to another.

Another generalisation, Isaac Newton's realisation that the force that pulled an apple to the ground and the force that kept the moon revolving around the earth was the same force, is one of the most useful generalisations in human history.

Hence generalisation can create new ideas out of old ones. No human ever saw a real giant yet the idea of giants arose in their minds by extrapolation from existing concepts—the concept of humans and the concept of things being different sizes. The first modern model of the atom was based very much on the solar system. X-ray diffraction photographs showed a nucleus with electrons orbiting around it. To 19th-century physicists the analogy was plain. Atoms were like little solar systems. The nucleus was like a little sun and the electrons were like little planets. Indeed the idea of atomic particles as little balls has persisted for almost 100 years although Quantum Theory characterises electrons not as little satellites at all but packets of energy orbiting the nucleus in a kind of spherical cloud. The more we analyse the particles of the nucleus, the more they appear to have no solidity at all.

And yet, in filling in the gaps in our knowledge we have no choice but to generalise from what we know. The galaxies appear to be flying apart in all directions. In our local precinct something that flies apart in all directions is characterised as an explosion, so the idea of the Big Bang has been postulated. Of course, if such a thing as the Big Bang occurred, it may have been nothing like an explosion as we understand it on earth but we cannot imagine things flying apart except as the result of an explosion, any more than ancient humans could understand how huge rocks could travel to the plain unless that they were thrown by gigantic creatures.

Concepts, however, can not only be extrapolated, they can be mixed and matched like pictures of animals in children's books in which the tops and bottoms can be combined in unusual ways. The properties of one concept can be applied to another, such as when a person uses a shoe to hammer a nail or when a person finds that the same mathematical formula applies to population growth in organisms as that used to calculate compound interest in banks, or when a person applies Darwin's theory of evolution to entities other than living creatures.

COMBINATION

Human beings are exposed, throughout their lives, to a variety of different doctrines. As I discussed in Chapter 2, people these days in the West, are confronted by a vast range of different propositions, different World Pictures. Because of the tendency to seek consistency, the individual's brain will naturally attempt to reconcile these different ideas into a coherent World Picture, a World Picture that seems to them to be free of contradictions.

An example might be a young child who is trying to reconcile the propositions transmitted by their parents with those transmitted by their peer group. It might be a scientist who is trying to reconcile different theories of physics, or psychology. In both cases a successful outcome might be a modified World Picture that contains elements of both ideas in a new combination.

This does not mean that all doctrines will be incorporated into the World Picture. As we have seen, doctrines that occupy the mind early in the piece often establish barriers—lock-out techniques which discredit ideas arriving later. The new ideas, as we know, can also employ strategies to get around the former doctrine's defences. Thus, a war is effectively waged in the mind of the individual for control of the World Picture.

In some cases the individual will live inside a society with such well-defended doctrines that they are never exposed to any alternative systems of thought. Members of a fundamentalist religious society in which all books, films and television are forbidden will hear very few ideas that contradict their existing ethos.

The more normal situation is the one I outlined in Chapter 2 whereby the individual continues to be exposed to ideas throughout their lives. In this situation doctrines are in a position to merge with each other, elements of one combining with elements of others, to constantly modify the World Picture. Sometimes these overall modifications will produce a set of propositions that seem to form a new body of thought, a set of ideas with their own definable character.

When we look closely at the great 'discoveries' of history, we find that the 'discoverers' were always steeped in different theories and information about their topic. We also find that many different people often come up with discoveries at about the same time. What this indicates is that in fact, people don't really make discoveries at all. New doctrines simply come into being in the brains of people who have absorbed other doctrines and made certain observations about the world around them. Given that there are always doctrines circulating around human society, it is not unlikely that the same set of doctrines will coincide and interact in the minds of several people at the same time, leading them to all formulate a new doctrine within the same passage of time.

Thus new ideas are constantly evolving in the minds of people. The evolution of ideas by combination also depends on the existence of human beings who have time to absorb a wide variety of doctrines. These are people who have traditionally been called scholars or academics, people who have time to read hundreds of books and hold extensive discussions with others. Such pursuits have been enabled by the agricultural and industrial systems that allow some members of the community to be full-time 'thinkers'. The evolution of ideas has accelerated rapidly since the development of agriculture some 5000 years ago and was accelerated even further with the advent of industrialisation some 200 years ago.

Thus, just as sexual reproduction produces a new and unique DNA strands, the combination of experience and ideas in the human mind produces new and unique relational propositions. These new propositions make up what we call 'our own point of view' and they are as unique to us as our DNA pattern is. They are a combination of all the influences to which we have been exposed in our life. In this way they are more complex than DNA. Sexual reproduction involves the combination of the DNA of two parents. A human mind may be influenced by thousands of different doctrines, propositions and tenets.

Herein lies another mechanism that accounts for the generation of new doctrines: the fact that people will interpret a proposition according to their own experience. As I pointed out in Chapter 3, language is something that puts the human brain into a particular state. However, it is implicit that no two brains, on being subjected to the same piece of language, will be put in exactly the same state. While people might use the same words, the meanings that those words engender will be unique to each person. This is because, as I have said earlier, meanings are made up of associations of recorded experiences including perceptions and feelings to which a verbal label has been attached. When I say the word 'uncle' to you, it induces a completely different set of images and associations from the ones it will induce if you say it to me.

It follows that not only will people associate words with different meanings, they will associate ideas with different events in their own World Picture. This can lead to new doctrines and propositions being generated quite unexpectedly. For example, at the end of the 19th century, a US electricity company conducted a demonstration for the government of New York during which they dramatically illustrated the dangers of the new power by electrocuting a dog. The distinguished members were mightily impressed, not just by the dangers of electricity but because the demonstration had solved a quite unrelated problem they had been grappling with, finding an efficient way to execute prisoners in New York's jails. And so the electric chair was born.

Doctrines will thus reconfigure themselves in the mind of each recipient according to the personal experiences and other doctrines that already make up the World Picture of that individual. They will also interact with and reconfigure those existing doctrines.

This book arose from my reading Richard Dawkins' *The Selfish Gene*, on explanation of the way in which DNA molecules employ species of biological creatures to perpetuate themselves. While reading the book I had the quite involuntary realisation that thought systems must be selected in the same way as biological systems. When I reached the end of the book I found that Dawkins had reached the same conclusion. On looking into the matter I have found that many other writers and researchers have formed similar opinions, both before and since. It is simply a matter of a certain combination of information and World Picture elements being present in an individual's mind at the same time.

The important thing about this process from a tenetic point of view is that the formulation of theories is usually regarded as the result of a conscious act by the thinker whereas tenetics would hold that the thinker has no control over it at all. They cannot help having the ideas. It was not, for example, any act of will that caused me to react to *The Selfish Gene* in the way I did. The book simply triggered a chain effect through my World Picture and I saw via generalisation that the mechanism that it proposed for the evolution of DNA molecules must apply to systems other than biological ones. The doctrine in this book has therefore evolved out of other doctrines before it. It is made up of biological evolutionary theory combined with cognitive psychology, sociology and other ideas. It is now attempting to reconfigure your view of the world, to create in your mind a new picture of how human society works. It is trying to create in your World Picture, an image of ideas, not as something abstract, but as almost living things, mechanisms engaged in a life-and-death struggle for their own survival, which are influencing human behaviour in the process. This book is therefore (like the parallel set of books on Meme Theory) to some extent, self-proving. It is an example of its own proposition that ideas transmit themselves in the form of books.

But you will put your own spin on the theory. You will relate the ideas in this book to your own experience and accept or reject its tenets according to the view of reality contained in your World Picture. You may think up some important modifications or refutations of the ideas. Whatever the case, unless your mind contains some powerful lock-out provision that rejects this whole theory, some version of the theory will now reside in your mind and you will probably at some time reproduce it, some part of it or some idea inspired by it in conversation, an essay, or perhaps a book of your own.

THE SELECTION OF DOCTRINES

A new and unique set of beliefs in the mind of an individual does not necessarily constitute a new doctrine, because it is not yet a self-sustaining, self-replicating system. As long as an idea exists in the mind of just one person it has no independent existence. However, from time-to-time, one of these new combinations of ideas may have the capacity to be transmitted to others especially if the person in whose mind the system appears is in a position to disseminate their opinions.

Not all doctrines will spread out and start to colonise other minds. It will only be some ideas that will have the instruction set that causes them to spread widely to others and once they do classic Darwinian processes come into play. Those ideas that are successful at infiltrating and reconfiguring the World Pictures of others will spread. Those that cannot do so effectively will die with their creators unless they are stored in some form whereby they can be reactivated later.

EMPIRICAL SELECTION

In 1960 psychologist Donald Campbell proposed a theory of 'blind' creativity. What Campbell suggested was that successful ideas do not come about through human intelligence but through the normal mechanisms of evolution— variation and selection. Looking back at humanity's history of famous authors, artists, composers and scientists, and the works and discoveries they produced, it is easy to stand in awe of the brilliance of the human mind. What we tend to forget is that the vast preponderance of books that are written, paintings that are painted and inventions that are devised never make it to the printing press, the gallery or the manufacturing plant.

What Campbell was proposing is that in any large population of people there will be a substantial number of people writing, composing, philosophising and inventing all the time. Of all the works produced those that society finds 'useful' are selected and reproduced. Retrospectively it will seem that those works were obviously the 'right' works, however this is only because we look at them in hindsight. If Shakespeare had never lived we would not miss him. We might instead revere another playwright who produced a different set of plays. There is nothing to suggest that *Hamlet* must inevitably have been written.

The same, however, does not apply to scientific discoveries and inventions. In the case of the physical sciences, it is only those theories and devices that seem to work that will survive, those that don't will be discarded. Again the traditional way of looking at scientific invention is to imagine an inventor cleverly working out what will work and building the invention accordingly. Campbell's view, which is the

Darwinian view, is that it is not so much the inventor as the universe that devises the theory or invention.

Imagine the following experiment. A roomful of people are given sheets of paper and told they have 3 hours to construct a paper plane that will glide 10 metres. The people all start folding and cutting the paper in certain ways. After half an hour they all line up and throw their planes and see which one travels furthest. Only one, Carlotta's plane, glides further than 5 metres. The people whose planes fall short or do not fly at all study the more successful planes and base their next round of designs on them. Some of them manage to improve on the design. By the third round, most of the group are making planes that fly 10 metres and one, Bart's, flies a remarkable 20 metres. The question is, who designed the winning plane? Was it Carlotta who came up with the first workable design or Bart who improved it? Or did the group design it collectively?

The Darwinian answer is that none of these is correct. The plane was designed by the laws of physics themselves, in the same way that the camel I described earlier was designed by the desert. The design of the final plane was determined by the force of gravity, the viscosity of air, the stiffness of paper, the design of the human forearm that throws the planes and so on. If any of these factors were different—say, the earth's atmosphere was less dense or paper was heavier—the final design would have been different. This is not to say that there is only one possible design of a paper plane but that the human designers do not have ultimate control over their invention. Their planes had to conform to the conditions of the environment in which they operate. The environment shaped their planes by causing the unfit planes to plummet to the floor. Thus environment shapes technology and science in the same way as it shapes a camel or a dolphin.

This process is what we might call empirical selection. It means that certain ideas—theories, inventions or whatever—are selected because they conform to the laws of this universe. When we conduct scientific experiments we are

simply exposing our ideas to empirical selection. We generate hypotheses and then see which ones are supported by
reality. Jumbo jets fly because we build them according to
a theory of aerodynamics that works. If it didn't work, planes
would fall out of the sky and we would have to modify the
theory and continue modifying it until it finally worked.
People employed in the area of technological design and
research will confirm that this is how knowledge and exper-
tise are gained, by a continual process of trial and error—the
errors being the ideas that are ruled out by the environment.
Empirical evolution is thus the most objective form of cognitive evolution we have, mainly because the selection
process is pretty much out of our hands. A plane either flies
or it doesn't and when a plane doesn't fly, it's pretty hard
to convince anyone that it does.

The notion that the universe shapes our knowledge is a
tantalising notion to people who want to ask the question
what is the human race or human knowledge evolving
towards? The post-Enlightenment view was that humans
were moving towards a state of perfection in which they
would be totally rational beings and live in an almost divine
state of harmony and reason. Events in the 20th century cast
doubts on this prognosis and, in the later decades of that
century, postmodernist philosophers saw fit to dismiss the
entire idea of human 'progress', maintaining that while things
change, they do not get any better. However, it is possible
to argue that through empirical evolution we are becoming
more and more 'fitted' to the universe. Through all the
thousands of scientific experiments and technological inventions, our knowledge of the workings of the universe is
constantly being broadened and deepened and this process
is being mediated by the universe itself. Empirical evolution
is slowly but surely steering us towards theories and practices
that are compatible with its underlying laws. Hence our
mental constructs are being gradually brought into line with
a set of external laws that preceded our presence in the
universe and were not tenetically created.

This view is based on the observation that, regardless of the power of doctrines to shape our view of reality, a doctrine cannot make a paper plane fly if the plane does not conform to the rules of physics. A doctrine can prevent us from trying to make paper planes, it can make us suppress or misreport the results of paper-plane experiments but it cannot actually alter the outcome of the experiment itself. A doctrine can, of course, cause us to interpret the cause or nature of the outcome in a different way but the results of the experiment itself will still be determined by the laws of the universe itself.

One of the implications of the idea of empirical selection is that presumably any organism, human or otherwise, that sets out to devise theories of how the universe works will discover the same principles. Martians trying to build spacecraft will converge towards the same formulae in relation to gravity, inertia and energy as human beings have. This is one of the more interesting hypotheses we will be able to test if we ever meet people from other worlds.

The idea of empirical selection is also demonstrated in the evolution of living creatures. We observe that animals of different genuses are capable of evolving towards the same shapes and behaviours despite possessing substantially different DNA. The dinosaur *struthiomimus*, looks like an ostrich: it is roughly the same height with a long neck, beak-like snout and two powerful legs for running. Its name (the *mimus* part means imitation) implies that it 'mimics' an ostrich though, of course, the dinosaur came first so, in fact, the ostrich should be called *sauromimus*.

We may find it extraordinary that two different animals, living 200 million years apart, should evolve such similar body shapes. The same convergence occurs between the shape of the ichthyosaur and the dolphin, and the triceratops and the rhinoceros. And there are contemporary examples. It is hard not to equate the hedgehog and the Australian echidna, small spiky creatures that roll themselves into a ball for protection. Except for the glaring exception that the echidna is one of the only two animals alive that lay eggs and suckle their young, they are almost exact equivalents. So, on the continent of Australia, isolated for long periods from the rest of the world, we find a creature that has evolved a form and a set of functions that almost exactly mimic a northern hemisphere species. We also note that the extinct Australian marsupial lion looked remarkably like a sabre-tooth tiger although its lineage is unrelated and far more ancient.

What this demonstrates is that biological entities converge towards forms that work regardless of their genetic heritage. Reptiles, birds and mammals have all evolved bipedal forms, forms with webbed limbs and the ability to dive, and forms that fly. Bats and pterosaurs both evolved a similar type of wing–skin stretched between elongated finger bones. It is no coincidence that whales and tuna have large flat tails for swimming. These features have been selected by the properties of water and air. Returning to our human examples we see that planes employ the same cross section of wing, whether they are made of canvas over wood or aluminium over titanium. It is the shape that works and the shape—or to be more specific, the *function* allowed by the shape— that is selected by the environment.

Just in case this gives the impression that this discussion is only concerned with matters relating to physics and chemistry, I should point out that social practices can also be validated by the fact that they 'work', at least for specific purposes. For example, the development of many of the social strategies outlined earlier such as property law, marriage, education and career specialisation can be empirically shown to correlate with a society's economic and military wealth. Also, powerful societies tend to be like one another. They have the same features—farms, ports, cities, laws, police, charities and schools. The traditional explanation (and the explanation offered by some Meme theorists) is that this occurs because of imitation. The Darwinian view would be that powerful civilisations are similar for the same reason that fish are similar: there are only a limited number of ways to *be* a powerful civilisation, there are only a certain number of configurations and strategies that work. Thus empirical selection or, to use Campbell's term, 'evolutionary episte-mology' converges tantalisingly towards the view of Voltaire's Dr Pangloss who believed we live in 'the best of all possible worlds'.

Before we take too much comfort from the idea of the 'universe' selecting our ideas, we should consider what happens in society when some of those factors that mould our ideas into ones that 'work' are removed.

REMOVING SELECTION

In the later stages of the 20th century we have seen a great disintegration of unity or belief. The Second World War enforced widespread doctrinal unity on the West. War is generally no time for political debate. The main task is survival and the doctrine that offers the best hope of survival— a doctrine of social uniformity, patriotism and common good—rapidly spreads through the society. (We can see concepts of national identity and togetherness that have been implanted since childhood become activated at the outbreak of conflict. Even today it is interesting to see how a military conflict can awaken a surprising degree of patriotic sentiment in people.)

The Western societies such as Britain, the United States and Australia came out of the Second World War with a strong sense of national unity and purpose. The sense of common good and common destiny flowed into peace time and the citizens of those nations addressed the creation of post-war wealth with the same unanimity that they addressed surviving the war. The result was a dramatic increase in economic wealth in the 1950s. By the 1960s, however, an entirely new generation had been born into this wealthy environment with no such sense of national unity of purpose.

The breakdown of traditional structures and traditions

in the 20th century has been linked to many social influences, such as increased mobility and the communications explosion, but the principle reason lies in the decline of selection mechanisms. In the absence of economic and military crises, alternative doctrines can arise because unanimity no longer has any social advantage. Much as church leaders, morals campaigners and science teachers may decry the decline in such things as life-long marriage and arithmetic, it is quite clear to many people that Western society has continued to operate with substantially reduced quantities of both these commodities. It is, for example, extremely hard to sell social practices that conserve human energy (such as monogamy and job specialisation) when human energy is surplus to requirements. The fact that people have leisure time—a product of the industrial age—and the fact that many people are unemployed demonstrates that we actually have more human energy than we need.

To put it bluntly, if people have time to watch television then it follows that they have time to engage in courtship behaviour with more than one mate, time to learn new jobs, time to change their place of residence and time to read about different belief systems. The sheer success of industrialisation, which transferred much of the demand for energy from humans to machines, has resulted in people 'courting' for longer—sometimes up to ten years—before getting married, more people leaving their marriage to resume dating or marry someone else, more people changing jobs or even switching career paths, people moving to different suburbs, cities or countries and the traditional, dominant doctrines of science and religion being substantially eroded by parapsychology, mysticism, earth cults, drugs, health fanaticism, self-help movements and occultism.

Decades of peace and wealth have removed the selection rules that previously eradicated such conspicuously unproductive and time-wasting practices. The result is the apparent paradox that, as Western culture has become more sophisticated technologically, it has become more gullible—that is to say, less empirical, intellectually.

This is of course at odds with how the philosophers of the Enlightenment saw human history unfolding. The 18th and 19th century view, an optimistic one as it has turned out, was that when humans were relieved of the burden of toil on farms, and in mines and factories, they would devote their new-found leisure time to the study of science and the arts. The world would then enter a golden age when humanity would become a race of philosophers, artists and explorers of the universe.

So what went wrong? First, let's not be too pessimistic. There are certainly more people going to school, reading, writing and studying than ever before. At the same time, however, Western culture has been inundated with intellectually meaningless pursuits—television, throwaway novels, arcade games, action films, spectator sports, disco music and the continuous acquisition of consumer items from clothes to appliances—that have rapidly sprung up to occupy the extra wealth and time industrialisation has created.

It is not the purpose of this book to enter into a detailed analysis of the tenetics of modern fashions and consumer movements. These have been dealt with exhaustively by writers such as James Brodie and Susan Blackmore. Here I will outline the general principle underlying the Enlightenment philosophers' mistake.

The luminaries of the 18th and 19th centuries saw toil and manufacture as stifling the intellectual development of humans. And indeed, in that labour did not allow time for intellectual pursuits, this was true. What they failed to see was that practical enterprises, such as farming, manufacturing and waging war, created a situation where empirical selection operated. As Samuel Johnson once said, the prospect of execution 'concentrates the mind wonderfully'. To put this in a broader context, in situations where our very existence is at stake only those propositions that actually work will be selected. People who are in critical situations—

that is, facing famine, war or economic threat—must formulate beliefs that result in working practical solutions. The scientific and social doctrines which existed in the early part of the 19th century existed because they produced tangible results.

The notion that practical outcomes determined the validity of a belief was expressed in the philosophy of pragmatism, a school of thought promulgated by the American philosopher and psychologist William James (brother of novelist Henry) among others. Its principle, reduced to the absolute minimum, is simply that things are true if they work. Propositions that produce observable results are selected and those that don't are discarded.

For thousands of years the need to effectively navigate, pump water, grow grain, fire catapults, create social stability, construct buildings, breed animals and so on had built up a substantial body of human knowledge, all the result of empirical selection. Most human beings were also engaged in practical activities on a daily basis. They baked bread, forged metal, sawed wood, sewed fabrics and engaged in other activities that continually validated or 'refreshed' their propositions about the world.

What the optimistic philosophers of the Enlightenment did not foresee was that in an industrialised world where people were less involved in the manipulation of their environment, where outcomes were not so critical, the selection process that weeds out working beliefs from non-working beliefs would become less effective. Hence, humans relieved of the anxiety of work and war, far from uncovering the secrets of the universe, would lose their ability to distinguish the real from the unreal.

While the trends in the later 20th century seem to bear out Donald Campbell's theory of evolutionary epistemology there are a couple of major problems with Campbell's theory. First, there is the problem that 'blind' selection cannot account for the rapid development of human knowledge. Blind selection means that variations arise completely at random, there is no 'intention' behind them at all. Just as genetic mutations are sheer accidents in replication, the ideas that are generated in the first place are completely random with no bias towards mutations that are advantageous. However, human thinking does not demonstrate this quality of total randomness. A seafarer seeking a route to the East Indies does not begin by placing pickles in a circle or knitting a sock. Nor need we assume that at some point in history some northern tribe experimented with the idea of setting fire to themselves to keep themselves warm at night, which resulted in the death of the tribe and the extinction of the idea.

Ideas are obviously subjected to some form of preselection at an internal level before they are submitted to experiment or social scrutiny.

OFF-LINE SELECTION

In the example of the paper planes we imagined a roomful of people trying out different shapes of paper plane until they developed something that flew a considerable distance. In a real 'blind' evolutionary situation, the people would start off making all sorts of random shapes—balls, squares, pieces of confetti—before they hit on anything that had something resembling wings or a tail. In our example the people started making something that 'looked' like a plane right from the beginning (because of generalisation).

In most human inventions, much of the selection occurs off-line—that is, inside the inventor's head—before a working model is made. What happens is the individual builds a mental model of the device and tests it against the existing tenets of their World Picture. Because the brain contains a model of the world it is possible to run simulations. In fact this is one of the main reasons for having a World Picture in the first place. The brain is a reality simulator. It is no co-incidence that one of the main uses of computers is to run simulations. It's because that's what humans do and computers are a mechanical extension of those processes.

Consider a person writing a book. They formulate a sentence, write it down, consider, realise that it does not make sense and cross it out. An individual considers a problem. In their mind they run a series of 'what-if' scenarios and consider the outcomes in what we might call an 'off-line' mode.

Thus we see a selection process where a new idea is selected by the prevailing doctrines inside the human head. The World Picture is a world in its own right, a cognitive world, and in it ideas are generated and selected. An individual trying to solve a problem or deciding on a course of action will consider several options. The mind automatically rules out many as impossible or inappropriate.

Imagine choosing a gift for someone. As you browse through the store and look at the range of items you may imagine the recipients opening the gift and looking at it. You might even imagine their reaction. If it is an item of homeware you might imagine their kitchen or bedroom and picture the gift on a shelf or the wall. If it is an item of clothing you might imagine them wearing it. In your internal world you will evaluate these images, 'No that doesn't go. That's not suitable'.

Thus thinking about something is a process in which the mind generates alternatives and then tests them in its own reality simulator. Ideas that fail in the simulator are discarded. To be a good ideas person you require two abilities. The capacity for divergence—the ability to generate a lot of different ideas—and convergence—the ability to select the best one, or select the best elements of each and put them together.

This is what happens when a group of people sit around trying to think up the answer to a problem. Someone makes a suggestion and the others say, 'No. That will never work'. What has happened here is that members of the group have run an instant simulation in their minds and seen that the proposal 'doesn't work' because it violates the principles within their model of the universe.

The answer that evolves in the end will be one that survives the natural selection process of passing through all the minds in the committee. This of course illustrates the principle problem with committees. Having more minds around a table can generate far more alternatives than just one. On the other hand, it's harder for any one idea to survive all those mental environments. The outputs of committees are often extremely unimaginative because the limit of innovation will be set by the least imaginative member of the group. To counter this, several proponents of creative thinking have proposed 'brainstorming' methods for group problem-solving. One of the rules of brainstorming[1] is that ideas are never rejected out of hand. No matter how silly an idea seems, it should be seriously discussed and developed for as long as possible. What brainstormers know is that an initial idea, while not being the answer in itself, may often lead on to a concept that does work. The rule of not dismissing any idea, no matter how silly it seems, thus has the effect of allowing ideas to evolve through more generations before being selected out. It increases the range of variations and makes it more likely that the group will end up with something that they could not have conceived when they started the discussion.

This entire process is often facilitated by having teams made up of divergent and convergent people. Divergence and convergence correspond to the evolutionary elements of variation and selection. Divergent people are those who come up with lots of ideas. Convergent people are those who are good at selecting the best bits of those ideas and putting them together.

Returning to selection within the individual brain, we are of course familiar with people who have little preselection ability. They are people who say the first thing that comes

---

1   The rules of brainstorming are another example of 'metarules'—rules about making rules.

into their heads. Much social behaviour—manners and tact for example—requires that utterances and actions be filtered by our off-line simulator before they are actually performed. People with poor reality simulation are likely to say the wrong thing at the wrong time. Their minds don't correctly test their utterances or their behaviours. On the opposite side are people who are insufficiently divergent. They are people whose doctrines are so fixed they generate almost no variations at all. This may be because they have a rigid view of reality that disallows any new concepts.

To summarise we can see that new ideas are selected by old ideas at three levels.

1. Individual level: any new proposition is assessed by the person's reality-testing procedures to see if it could be true or could work.

2. Social level: once the individual forms an opinion as to the validity of the idea they expose it to others. The other people express their opinion—based on their own truth-testing systems. In the committee situation this is when people say, 'That will never work', 'The problem is . . .' or 'That's great. Why didn't I think of that?'. Ideas are regularly subjected to this kind of filtration in families, work places and government.

3. Institutional level: doctrines establish institutional structures to promulgate their own tenets. Should an idea, which is contrary to the doctrines, be accepted by an individual mind and then be accepted by a social group, the institutions have mechanisms including police, courts, schools and doctors ready to deal with it.

The second problem with Campbell's theory is that if ideas were selected because they 'worked', then things would work a lot better than they do. People would not believe things that are obviously untrue. Computers would never crash. Trains would arrive on time. I would be able to program my video recorder.

The trouble is that the Campbellian view does not take into account the way in which doctrines affect the testing process. While planes do fly and specialised societies do build powerful civilisations, the world is full of propositions that are not empirically selected at all. They have been selected, both in the individual mind and society, by other ideas that have evolved powerful strategies for their own survival. Ideas that are incompatible with these existing doctrines are written off as 'unworkable', 'impractical', 'misguided', 'dangerous', 'insane' and so on. This is partly because not all ideas are amenable to empirical selection. In the next chapter we will see why.

CHAPTER 9

THE PROOF ZONE

ALL HUMAN EXPERIENCE IS recorded in the form of connections in the brain. This pattern of connections forms the World Picture of the individual. It contains the sum total of the individual's memories and learning. It is their internal map of the world and the record of their own existence.

Prior to the development of spoken language all this experience was obtained first hand by the individual. Young animals learn either through imitation—they watch others performing actions and then copy them—or by practice. Young lions and wolves accompany their parents on hunting expeditions. Macaque monkeys 'show' their young how to crack open crab shells by pounding them with rocks. Peregrine falcons 'teach' their young to hunt by carrying dead birds up into the sky and dropping them so the young can practice plucking their prey out of the air.

We know that both these learning techniques are vital. Contrary to our traditional theories of 'instinct', young lions who do not accompany their elders on the hunt grow up to be poor hunters. Baby monkeys who are taken from their mothers at an early age turn out to be bad mothers because they have never seen mothering in action. We also know that we cannot teach a child to ride a bicycle by talking about it or drawing a diagram. The child has to get on the bike and learn by trial and error.

Through imitation and practice individuals learn about the relationships between cause and effect, for example, hitting a crab with a rock can break the shell and expose the edible parts. This is a kind of non-verbal proposition ('hitting crabs with rocks leads to breaking the shell, which leads to getting the meat') that exists as a memory stored physically in the brain and a set of neural paths which, when required, will take the individual back to that memory. It does not exist in any symbolic or linguistic form but is basically just a record of perceptions. Nevertheless it is in its own way a cause-and-effect equation. A child who sees an older sibling drag a chair over to reach the cupboard where the cake is kept, immediately makes a new addition to their library of cause-and-effect associations. A child learning to ride a bike is learning, or rather the motor-section of their brain is learning, that if they lean this way, the bike goes that way. The result is that—even though it may not be a conscious perception—some permanent record of actions and outcomes is stored. These learned connections about causes and effects, and correlations between events, are what we might call relational concepts. Two concepts are linked together in some sort of relationship: this causes that, he has this, I want that.

Although imitation and practice are the earliest forms of human learning and occurred in animals long before the evolution of humans, they still correspond to the most reliable scientific methods that we have today. Imitation (learning by watching) and practice (learning by doing) correspond to the two pillars of scientific investigation: observation and experiment. It is a theme that I will keep coming back to in this book: science is not an invention of civilisation nor is it derived from systems of abstract reasoning, but is an inevitable development of the way in which living creatures naturally learn.

From a tenetic point of view the important thing about imitation and practice is that they are verifiable forms of learning. That is, you know you have learned to ride a bike when you find yourself actually riding it. You know that hitting the crab shell with the rock works when your parent scoops out the crabmeat and hands it to you. What this reveals to us is that verifiable knowledge—what we can also call empirical knowledge—preceded the development of symbolic language by millions of years, and is not dependent on it.

This does not mean, however, that symbolic language is a recent development in the animal world. Language has long been used by animals on earth but not for communicating stored experience. Rather it has been used for communicating information about immediate circumstances. Prairie dogs, for example, warn other members of the colony of the approach of predators by making loud squeaks and chirps. These noises are a code with different squeaks and chirps representing different types of predator. Note that this is a genuine symbolic code because the squeaks in no way seek to imitate the 'look and feel' of the predator. The prairie dogs do not perform an imitation of the predator. They have a language made up of signals which bear no similarity in sound or form to what they represent. This is the criterion of a real language.[1]

Most mammals issue both verbal and visual signals to indicate a state of mind—submissive, aggressive, sexually interested and so on. Early humans no doubt had a capacity to indicate the current situation, both external and internal, by means of coded sounds. We might imagine that the first human words probably expressed emotional states, feelings

---

1   Humans make this transition when, as toddlers, they graduate from calling a dog a 'woof woof' to a 'dog'. The word 'dog' in no way resembles the sound made by a dog. You cannot deduce what it means by listening to it, you have to know what the word means. This is the basis of semantic or symbolic language as opposed to mimetic or imitative language. The same distinction applies to writing based on an alphabet as opposed to hieroglyphics or little pictures.

or needs: 'food', 'water', 'enemies', 'stop', 'go', 'danger' and 'hunger'. However, sometime during the last half million years, the use of language underwent a significant change when our ancestors developed the ability to use symbolic language to transmit relational concepts. This development, the ability to use a symbolic code to communicate the results of their own learning rather than just simple expressions of their current state, was to totally change the course of human development.

First, it freed up an enormous amount of human energy. It was no longer always necessary to perform actions in order to learn something. Whereas once a human being had to walk to the end of the valley to find out what was there, another human could now say 'I've been to the end of the valley and there is a river there'. Second, it created a new realm of non-empirical knowledge. The effect of this can be illustrated by considering how a human child develops its knowledge of the world.

NON-VERBAL LEARNING

The construction of our World Picture occurs through the following steps:

- *Sensory experience.* The individual experiences a constant stream of sensations from their perceptual and their emotional systems.

- *Perceptual interpretation.* In the cortex these raw sensations of sound, light and touch are organised into entities such as shapes, textures and noises.

- *Concept formation.* A set of perceptions is organised into a Gestalt—an entity recognisable as a separate and distinct thing in itself. For example, a set of perceptions that includes barking, furriness, doggy smell, jumping up and wetness on the face becomes the experience of a single entity, something that—if we knew English—we would call a dog. I will call the non-verbal version of this animal a (dog). Experience of several dogs may lead to a general concept of (dogs), which I will notate as [dog]. A [dog] has the properties of a (dog) but is not any one specific (dog).

Relational concepts

Individual concepts are linked together to form a network of associations that forms our World Picture. The World Picture contains not just the concept of (dog) but the relational concept that (Grandma) has a (dog), that there is a (dog) in the (house next door), that the (dog) is eating his (dinner). It also contains relational concepts regarding our own actions and certain experiences. If we (pat) the (dog) it (licks) our (hand). Generalisation extends from specific relational concepts—this (dog) has (ears)—to general relational concepts—[dogs] have [ears].

These relational concepts fall into two categories: perceptual association, or concepts of what things are like, and operational associations, or concepts of how to do things. Not coincidentally, these categories, relate to the two different types of computer program content, data and instructions, and they also reflect the two basic scientific processes: observation and experiment. Perceptual association concepts answer the questions 'What?', 'Where?' and 'When?' and operational association concepts answer the question 'How?'.

These processes can occur without social assistance. The brain simply performs these organisations as part of its function. Indeed a brain must perform these functions or behaviour and survival would not be possible. Gestalts are necessary to maintain a sense of continuity in our perception. If our perceptions were not organised into such entities, we could not recognise anything in the world from minute to minute. Simply turning a dog around or seeing it in a different light would make it appear to be a different object. Of course, this can still happen when we see something in a light in which we've never seen it before. Even meeting a person outside their usual surroundings can cause us to forget who they are—a reminder that the attributes of an object include things such as location and function as well as colour, height and so on. However, humans and other animals would have died out aeons ago if they failed to recognise their mate or their home just because they saw them from a different angle.

The only time entities seem to lose their continuity is when we are dreaming. When we are asleep, the rules of identity or object persistence seem to be suspended. Trains turn into boats and then into fish and into plates and then into shoes without disturbing us. It seems that when we are asleep, because the perceptual mechanisms that process information from the outside world are turned off, we simply do not require our sensations to be consistent. However, dreaming while you are awake can be an alarming if not terrifying experience. People suffering from hallucinatory disorders and people who take drugs that disrupt perception may go into panic as they experience perceptions that no longer make sense. Objects do not retain their identity from moment to moment, perceptions of shape, distance and even colour alter, and entities appear out of context. In its waking state our brain's 'mapping' system tries to find the rules in this new world and cannot. The result is fear.

This leads to an important observation. The fact that mental illness and hallucinatory drugs can alter perceptions shows that our perceptual processes and concepts, and our conceptual associations, are not set in stone. A new set of perceptions can, temporarily at least, totally alter our view of the world. In severe conditions that view can be permanently disrupted. This suggests that during our daily experience our reality is continually being renewed or 'refreshed'— a term now commonly used for the rapid reloading of the image on a computer monitor—by our sensory input.[2]

---

2 Earlier I referred to the continual verification of some propositions by daily experience as constantly 'refreshing' the validity of the idea.

VERBAL LEARNING

Although formation of these concepts can occur without social assistance they usually don't. In human society the process of concept formation occurs in conjunction with the learning of language. This occurs through the following stages:

- *Labelling.* A child sees its first (dog). An adult immediately names the furry barking entity 'dog' or 'doggie'. The concept (dog) is now neurally associated with the word 'dog'. From now on when someone says 'dog' the child will think of (dog) or [dog].

- *Concept translation.* Most early language training is mediated by the parents' maintaining a running commentary about things in the child's life. Thus, over time, the adult translates the child's developing relational concepts into linguistic form: 'Look, the doggie's barking', 'Pat the doggie' or 'Don't lick me dog'.

- *Reportage.* In time the child learns to form their own propositions, in the form of sentences, based on their experiences and concepts. 'The doggie licked me', 'The doggie is running' or 'The doggie is sad'. So far so good. Now here comes the change.

- *Propositional input.* The adult introduces new concepts that have not been directly experienced by the learners, 'Be careful, the doggie might bite'. The input of this relational proposition creates a new concept for the child that has not been derived from their own learning. The child may never have never been bitten by a dog, nor seen a dog bite anyone, but a connection between 'doggie' and 'bite' is now established. The proposition 'dogs bite' is now part of their World Picture. We might assume that this is a different kind of concept because it arrives in the form of words rather than personal experience. However, because the word 'dog' evokes the concept

of [dog]—and this dog in particular—and the word 'bite'
evokes the concept of [being bitten], the new mental
association between [dog] and [bite] can be as strong as
if were derived from an actual memory. In fact received
propositions can be stronger than concepts based on
association because they go straight to the generalised
level of knowledge. This explains how an individual can
hate homosexuals in general, but quite like their friend
Bob even though he's gay.

Of course, a child who has never been bitten may
have no concept such as 'being bitten' and the proposition will be meaningless. Any word—except those with
implicitly abstract functions—that cannot be traced back
to some sort of experience will be devoid of meaning,
but a child who has had the experience of being bitten
by anything—an ant or another child—is likely to pull
their hand away.

- *Reiteration*. Subsequently the child may even pass on
  the proposition to another child—'The doggie might
  bite you'—even though the proposition has never been
  corroborated by an actual nip.

It is quite easy to see the advantage of verbal learning. As
I have explained above, it spares the individual from having
to learn everything through experience. The child does not
have to suffer a bite in order to learn. The disadvantage
is equally obvious. Symbolically transmitted propositions are
not necessarily true. Thus, while on the one hand the development of symbolic communication created an enormous leap
in efficiency for human beings, it also created a number of
dangers. For the first time, the possibility of deception or
misinformation entered the human learning process.

While observation and experiment are slow, they tend
to be reliable. It is very unlikely that a young animal will
learn the wrong thing by watching its parents and quite
unimaginable that an animal would deliberately falsify its
behaviour to mislead its young. Indeed, unless you are a

professional conjurer, falsifying a physical demonstration requires considerable effort. On the other hand, a symbolic proposition can be altered with little or no expenditure of energy. The human in our first example can change matters considerably by saying, 'I've been to the end of the valley and there is no river there', knowing that there is. Or a human can tell their colleague that there is fresh water at the end of the valley knowing full well that there is actually a hungry lion waiting there.

Of course, there is no obligation on the part of the learner to trust any particular symbolic communication and we can expect that people will often decide to test propositions by direct experience. The listener can walk to the end of the valley and find out if the speaker is telling the truth. Nevertheless, the development of the symbolic transmission of propositions created, for the first time, the possibility that an animal could form relational concepts in its brain that are not based on experience, something which was previously almost impossible.

The problem is symbolic communication is just as capable of transmitting concepts that are records of experience (memories) as concepts that have been manufactured within the brain by generalisation, imagination or some other form of idea creation.

Symbolic communication is also subject to reiteration— the process whereby people simply repeat propositions without testing them for validity. Unless a listener was prepared to test every proposition personally, which of course negates the whole advantage of the system, there is no way of establishing the truth of transmitted information other than making some assessment of the reliability of the speaker.

Therefore an evolutionary principle came into operation: whether these symbolically encoded propositions were copied from brain to brain depended not on whether they were true or not, but whether they appeared to be true—an important distinction.

In order for a proposition to appear to be true, it may need no other credentials than the fact that it is uttered by a person who commands some respect—such as a parent. Of course if the proposition conflicts with observable reality—if the speaker proposes that there is no river at the end of the valley and the listener walks to the end of the valley and finds that there is a river—not only is the proposition discredited, but the speaker is as well.

On the other hand, if it is a statement that *cannot be disproved by observation or experiment*, then the respectable status of the speaker could be enough to carry the day. This takes us back to the situation in Chapter 2 where we saw that children will believe in Santa Claus, because they trust their parents and they have no means of testing the proposition.

The result of humans developing verbal communication is that we now find culture to be a mixture of verifiable propositions derived from everyday processes and unverifiable propositions related to events to which we have little or no access. Interestingly, this situation seems to have come about almost immediately with the development of symbolic language. If we look at the oldest existing tribal cultures on earth we find that their culture is a mixture of extremely sophisticated knowledge in relation to their immediate environment, toolmaking, food preparation, animal behaviour, biological processes and so on, and extremely inaccurate (though often very elaborate) concepts relating to matters historically and geographically beyond their capacity to test: the structure and creation of the earth, the nature of the stars and the mechanisms behind the seasons or the weather.[3]

The striking thing is that many of these propositions have remained, to the best of our knowledge, unchanged for up

---

3   It is interesting to note that in hunter–gatherer societies, physical behaviour is still transmitted primarily by demonstration and imitation. Parents show their children how to weave, throw spears or dig for yams. Spoken language is reserved for the more abstract and unphysical concepts such as laws, history and religion.

to 50 000 years, prompting the question of how propositions not based on any first-hand evidence can survive intact over such vast periods of time.

One way of explaining this is to say that people have a 'proof zone'. This is the area of human experience inside which it is possible to test and verify propositions. Our proof zone is defined as our maximum range of interaction with the physical world. Beyond the proof zone it is not possible to test or verify propositions so we must rely on conjecture, induction, deduction or statements made by authority figures. In the case of the child, a question as to whether or not there is cake in the cupboard lies inside their proof zone, but the question as to whether or not there really is a Santa Claus lies outside it. For a tribe of nomadic hunter–gatherers, knowledge about how to find and prepare food or how to cure diseases lies within the proof zone. However, questions about the nature of the stars or what causes disease (in the sense of bacteria and viruses) lie outside the proof zone.

The distinction is that propositions relating to matters inside the proof zone are capable of being verified whereas propositions regarding matters outside the proof zone are not able to be verified. Both types of proposition are capable of surviving in transmitted culture, but for quite different reasons. Propositions within the proof zone persist because they are capable of being verified by experience and continue to be verified by experience. On the other hand, propositions outside the proof zone cannot be disproved and hence they may never be directly discredited. Thus there are two quite different reasons why a proposition continues to remain 'intact', that is not disproved.

1. The proposition continues to be verified by experience.
2. The proposition lies outside the proof zone.

This leads me to one of our tenetics' most important principles:

24. Propositions will tend to be transmitted until they are disproved, therefore propositions that cannot be disproved can be transmitted indefinitely.

TENETICS' IMPACT ON GENETICS

From the point that verbal transmission of information developed it is likely that doctrines became a significant force in the shaping of human DNA. For example, given that doctrines were transmitted by symbolic language, a priority for any doctrine would have become the eradication of humans who could not understand and replicate the doctrine. For a start, other groups of hominids who could not share experience through language were probably wiped out.[4] Then, within Homo Sapiens, individuals who had less ability to retransmit symbolic ideas were probably eliminated since they represented competition for valuable resources with those humans who were capable of reproducing the doctrine.

This process is still observable today with the eradication, or confinement, of people who are 'unteachable', 'uncivilised' or 'bestial'. Individuals who, for whatever reason, are not influenced by transmitted doctrines but controlled by their in-built urges and instincts are regarded as a threat to society. For the last few thousand years such people have been jailed and executed. Their 'crime' is essentially not being susceptible to doctrines, behaving instead according to innate instincts like a pre-verbal animal. Since the doctrines cannot 'occupy' the cognitive structures of these people, they remove them from society.

The evolution of ideas has therefore had an effect on the evolution of human beings by 'selecting' humans who are more likely to adopt—and transmit—doctrines. It is little wonder that a three-year-old human is capable of learning

---

4   It is now believed that several different strains of proto-humans co-existed in the world prior to the dominance of the Homo Sapiens.

ten new words a day. Humans who have trouble learning language and therefore cannot easily be indoctrinated have tended to be 'selected out'. The result is that, since doctrines first appeared, human beings have become more adept at language and able to handle more complex doctrines.

Pessimists might hypothesise that, since doctrines are threatened by reality testing, they have also methodically worked to eliminate people who tend toward empiricism, people who base their beliefs on what they see for themselves rather than what they're told. Most certainly it would be in the interests of all doctrines to populate the world with people who readily believe what they are told.

At any rate, individuals in whose hearts and minds doctrines are unable to harness themselves tend to be separated out and confined. These individuals are commonly called 'criminals', or are characterised as 'incorrigible' or 'intransigent' and are locked up, executed or in other ways neutralised. Psychologists may even diagnose these humans as 'psychopaths' or 'sociopaths' meaning that they are unusually immune to the teachings of the surrounding society and tend to do whatever they feel like at the time. Interestingly, a common insult hurled at such people is that they are 'animals', in other words, creatures beyond the reach of doctrines.

Whatever the relationship between genetic and tenetic evolution, it is the latter that has been the more important process over the last 10 000 years. The present state of the world is the result of the evolution of doctrines rather than the physical evolution of humans.

CHAPTER 10

TESTING, TESTING

WHAT I HAVE PROPOSED in Chapter 9 is that there are areas in our model of reality that are outside the proof zone and that in areas where propositions cannot be tested by empirical selection, our World Picture will tend to be filled by doctrines that are plausible. In this context, 'plausibility' refers to the tenetic strength of the doctrine, meaning its ability to become incorporated into the existing World Picture of the individual.

However, we should not fall into the trap of imagining that all propositions within the proof zone are subject only to empirical selection. As I discussed in Chapter 8, new ideas are filtered through existing ones and doctrines are capable of eliminating competing systems of thought. Basically, doctrines shape our World Picture in two ways: first, by the imposition of language and second, by controlling the rules of logic that we apply.

THE POWER OF LANGUAGE

As we have seen, language is not just a means of communicating thoughts and feelings, it is the means of organising our memories and experiences so that people will behave in certain ways. In fact most of our knowledge consists of other people's memories, thoughts and experiences, which have been coded and packaged into linguistic forms.

Although children have a remarkable aptitude for language and, according to the linguist Noam Chomsky, the rules of syntax are genetically coded in the mind,[1] the action of coding experiences as words does not happen automatically.

As I discussed earlier, the original purpose of language was to express emotions and warnings rather than concepts or actions. The first utterances made by children convey hunger, anger, happiness and pain, and it is only through conditions imposed by the parents that the child learns that they must use names for objects if they want their needs to be met. It is not uncommon to find children as old as two or three still asking for things by crying or grunting and pointing at the object in question. If the parent responds and actually hands the object to the child, this sort of behaviour can continue for some time. What most parents do is refuse to hand over the toy or the food until the child names the object. The child has to learn to say 'ball' or 'drink' before they get what they want. Thus, as we saw in Chapter 2, the child learns not only how to name things but the importance of naming things. The child learns that everything has a name—although this is not really true—and learns those names according to their parents' rules.

Later on they will learn to name things according to the rules imposed by their teachers, the church, television, their peer group and so on. The naming of phenomena is not an emotionally neutral activity. While naming objects is generally a pragmatic exercise, when we move into the area of naming actions and qualities, language becomes emotional or value laden. Words such as 'right', 'wrong', 'good', 'bad', 'rude',

---

1   This is understandable given that the syntax of language developed out of, and reflects, the syntax of non-verbal thinking, which existed for millions of years before human language appeared.

'nice', 'naughty', 'dirty', 'correct' and 'incorrect' have emotional implications for the child. 'Good', 'nice', 'right' and so on are associated with parental approval, whereas 'bad', 'naughty' and 'wrong' are associated with disapproval. Later on these simple approval or disapproval words will include more complex terms such as 'moral' and 'immoral', 'responsible' and 'irresponsible', 'honour' and 'dishonour', 'righteousness' and 'sin', and 'justice' and 'injustice'. These types of words have two characteristics. One, as we have said, is that they carry emotional implications—positive or negative. The other is that the definitions of these words are not fixed. They vary greatly between families and cultures. What is regarded as 'honourable' in one culture, for example, avenging an insult to the family, is regarded as 'criminal' or 'vindictive' in another. What might be regarded as 'romantic' in one country, for example, two young lovers eloping, might be regarded as 'sinful' and 'dishonourable' somewhere else. Even within a single culture we differentiate between similar occurrences by assigning particular words to them. For example the act of killing can be variously described as 'murder', 'manslaughter', 'execution', 'retribution' or 'euthanasia'. Debate over issues such as capital punishment and euthanasia primarily revolve around pinning a particular label to the act—opponents of both argue that they constitute 'murder'. It is as if winning the argument over the label constitutes winning the argument over the act. Indeed, most of what happens in courts of law is concerned with fitting the right label to an event. If the judge or jury ends up labelling the act 'theft', 'fraud' or 'murder', the results for the plaintiff or defendant will be vastly different from if they label it 'borrowing', 'honesty' or 'self-defence'.

In short, doctrines can influence our view of reality by manipulating the definitions of words. Words are capable of motivating people to extreme actions such as killing, imprisoning or ostracising others. To motivate human beings to perform certain actions, a doctrine can redefine words and apply them to any activity that the doctrine wishes to reward or punish. To the people operating within a culture, the meanings of these words are not arbitrary assignations, they represent reality. Thus, people do not call a person who has been found guilty of murder in a court 'someone a jury defined as having committed an act of murder' but 'a murderer'.

The word 'murderer' is used by laypeople and media as if it were an objective description for a person, like 'electrician' or 'plumber', when in fact it is far more culturally determined. An individual who blows up a building in peacetime killing 100 people is a 'murderer' whereas as one who blows up an enemy building during a war, killing 100 people, is a 'hero'.

A similar process happens with the word 'criminal', which is perceived by most people as representing a state of reality—that a particular person is a criminal—rather than a provisional label. And yet, a person can be changed from criminal to non-criminal by simply changing a law. If a government passes a law 'decriminalising' the use of a particular drug, the people using that drug are overnight transformed from being criminals to non-criminals. The person, and even the act they perform, is the same, and yet they are no longer classified as criminals. Conversely, by making an act, such as owning an unregistered machine gun, a criminal offence, people who were previously not criminals are redefined as criminals. Thus, the state of being a criminal can be determined by the prevailing laws of the land, and yet many people regard criminality as a characteristic of the individual—something which exists in the person regardless of the surrounding culture.

However, it is not just the idea that words reflect 'reality' that is deceptive, but the very notion that all words have meanings at all. The effect of the naming game in childhood is that, in general, individuals come to believe that every object or event has a corresponding word, and every word represents some object or event. However, in everyday life, there are many words that do not have any clearly definable meaning, not even the socially imposed labels described in the previous paragraphs.

Words that sound impressive but defy any practical definition, such as the 'grace of God', are frequently used in religion. Theologians have written hundreds of pages of text discussing what grace means, what it does not mean and what its implications are, ignoring the fact that if a word's meaning is not apparent there is probably no point in using it at all.

In the case of ordinary language we might consider the word 'average', a word constantly used by politicians and lobby groups in reference to the 'average family' or the 'average man'. While the word 'average', which technically refers to a set of mathematical measures of tendency, can be applied to numerical data, it is virtually impossible to apply it to phenomena such as human beings. The average of the numbers 2, 3, 5 and 6 is 4 which is a meaningful average in the sense that 4 is a real number. However, the average family is but an imaginary concept. We may calculate that a family has an average income, or an average number of children (though even these calculations yield different results according to the method you use) but we cannot define any existing family, or number of families, as being 'average' in any meaningful way. We can only look at averages in relation to specific questions such as 'average expenditure on milk' or 'average days of illness'. Even then, the figure arrived at will depend on a whole series of definitions and formulae all of which can significantly affect the outcome. Still politicians, lobby groups and survey companies throw around 'average' figures as if they represented some sort of reality.

The word 'average' can even give misleading results in a purely mathematical context. The concept of 'average wages', for example, gives no real idea of how much people earn, because the incomes of a few super-wealthy individuals yank the average up above what most people make.

Much of the current discussion over climate change

revolves around calculated rises in 'average' world temperatures even though the concept of an 'average global temperature' has no real meaning. Obviously, the temperature of the earth varies all over its surface, not only from place to place, but also from moment to moment. Temperatures vary from morning to night, from winter to summer, according to altitude, latitude and prevailing weather conditions. To make any sort of accurate calculation of 'average', be it the mathematical mean, median or mode, would require literally millions of thermometers located over the entire surface of the globe from the bottom of the ocean, to the tops of mountains, even floating in balloons through the atmosphere, with measurements taken every hour, on the hour, for years on end. Even so, simply averaging the readings would tell us very little about climatological trends. What we would be more interested in would be increasing extremes in temperature, changes in the range of temperature, or the pattern of temperature. Even then we could not make any definitive pronouncements about whether the earth was getting warmer since the fluctuations in heat continuously vary in both small patterns and large patterns (what we call a fractal pattern) over vast periods of time. Yet greenhouse and anti-greenhouse proponents alike argue about changes in 'average' temperatures.

My purpose is not argue one way or the other about the state of global warming, the grace of God or the morality of bombing but simply to show that many terms, even apparently 'scientific' terms, are linguistic artefacts that affect the individual's perception of what is real. Beyond language, however, there are other cognitive mechanisms that influence what we see as true or false.

CAUSE AND EFFECT

As I have said earlier, one of the processes that doctrines control is the organisation of perceptions into recognisable patterns. One of the most important of those patterns is cause and effect. Cognition evolved in the first instance as an aid to survival. Its primary purpose is to allow an organism to make predictions which will be right most of the time. In Chapter 9 I grouped relational concepts in two groups: perceptual associations, which are concepts about what things are like ('facts'); and operational associations, which are about how things work ('principles'). The difference is that while our knowledge of facts tell us how things are, operational associations allow us to conjecture what will happen in novel or unknown situations.

Operational associations or principles are basically cause-and-effect propositions that allow us to predict that, 'If we do A, then B will happen, or tend to happen'. 'If I drop this egg on the floor it will break. If I am late for work I will probably be reprimanded.'

Because cause-and-effect propositions are the basis of making predictions and therefore vital to our survival, they have long been central to human World Pictures. It is therefore little wonder that much social and political debate centres around arguments to the effect that if we allow one thing to occur then other things will flow from that: rock and roll music will lead to widespread immorality in the young, the use of fossil fuels will lead to irreversible global warming, legalising prostitution will lead to a collapse of the family or legalising heroin will lead to a reduction in drug-related crime. Advocates of both reform or the status quo will also not only seek to make predictions based on such cause-and-effect propositions but will seek to attribute causes to current events, arguing that divorce rates are a result of the rise of feminism, that unemployment is a result of economic rationalism or the spread of AIDS is due to a breakdown in 'morality'.

History, sociology and politics have become 'cause' industries, not in the sense of supporting causes, but in the sense of trying to establish causes for social phenonema, a tendency that has led to vast numbers of largely debatable cause-and-effect relationships being postulated. This is quite understandable in the context of the modern world when we realise that, as governments have come to spend more money on social policies regarding welfare, education, health and social security, the question of the 'outcomes' of these policies have become a matter of great financial and political concern. Thus, social scientists and researchers have turned their efforts increasingly to trying to understand the 'causes' of illiteracy, delinquency, marriage breakdown, unemployment and other phenomena, with a view to finding solutions. The dilemma is that in many of these cases it is impossible to categorically define any 'cause' at all. There may be many conditions that are associated with each other, such as lack of education and poverty with unemployment, but it is difficult to define which of these factors are 'causes' and which are 'effects' since they co-exist simultaneously.

Economists, particularly in the 20th century, have set out to try and formulate rules of cause-and-effect, many of which have been adopted, sometimes fanatically, by adherents of both right- and left-wing politics. Sociology and psychology have also entered the arena, making many predictions in relation to issues such as poverty, single-parent families, education and child care.

Despite a century of theory and research in these areas, most predictions in relation to human society do not work and the cause-and-effect relationships postulated apply only in retrospect. For example, we can show that a great number of child-abusers were themselves abused as children but we do not know, and have no way of finding out, how many children who are abused grow up to be child-abusers. Hence, we cannot make any confident prediction regarding the probability of any one abused child growing up to be an abusing parent.

The problem is aggravated by the fact that even if we can establish a statistical connection between types of events, it does not mean that there is a causal connection. Indeed, to a great extent, the entire concept of causality is an artefact of human cognition caused by an extrapolation (generalisation) from our own action associations ('If I do this, that will happen'). However, because these are so central to our survival and so inculcated into us as children ('if you touch that it will electrocute you') we tend to look for cause and effect in all events in life—even where it may not exist—and we will tend to mistake things such as contiguity (two things happening in spatial or temporal proximity to each other) and correlation (two things occurring in regular association with each other) as showing a cause-and-effect relationship. This tendency allows doctrines containing cause-and-effects tenets to gain credence, even when the purported relationship is quite illusory.

To illustrate how misleading the sense of cause-and-effect can be, let us consider the techniques of some professional, though not necessarily intentional, illusionists. Professional magicians or conjurers exploit ambiguities in the perception of reality and causality every day. They appear to do the impossible: make birds appear and disappear, or make people vanish and reappear in boxes. The people in the audience know they are being fooled—they know that the girl is not really sawn in half—and yet their senses are still fooled. An uneducated person taken to a magician's show might quite possibly believe that a living person was cut in half and restored by the magician.

These days, there are two firm unwritten laws in regard to magicians. One is that they never reveal their techniques, the other is that they never pretend that they are really doing magic. In ancient times this was not the case. The tricks were perceived, and intended to be perceived, as genuine.

Sometimes in the modern world, magicians break the rules and claim that they are really doing magic. Such a magician was an illusionist called Uri Geller, a professional conjurer who began claiming to be able to perform genuine psychic 'miracles', including bending spoons and starting stopped watches. He was soon touring the world performing his tricks on television and making much more money than if he had remained a simple conjurer working the nightclubs.

One area Geller exploited was people's unfamiliarity with large numbers. Geller would appear on television and ask the people watching the show at home to go and find an old watch that had stopped working years ago. Then he would claim that, using his mind, he could restart some of those watches. He would pretend to concentrate and minutes later hundreds of people would ring the television station to say that their watches had started ticking after being stopped for years. What Geller knew was that watches that have been stopped for years will occasionally start to move if they're picked up and held—sometimes because of the movement, sometimes because of the warmth of the hand. He also knew that millions of people were watching the live broadcast. Statistically, if only one in 100 viewers went to get a watch (1 per cent) and only one in 100 of those watches (1 per cent of 1 per cent or one in 10 000) started ticking when they were picked up, that still would amount to hundreds of watches—enough to make the TV station switchboard light up.

It seems miraculous but when you are dealing with numbers as large as millions, extremely rare events (even things that are a 1:10 000 chance) not only become possible, they become a certainty.

A famous financial scam runs as follows: a con man prints up two bogus financial newsletters and mails them to a list of 1600 rich people selected from a magazine such as *Fortune*. In one newsletter he predicts that a certain stock will rise in value: in the other half he predicts that the same stock will fall. This means, whatever happens, 800 of the newsletters will be correct, the other 800 will be incorrect. A month later the con man checks the stock prices and sends out another newsletter to the 800 people who got the correct prediction. Again he sends out two versions: 400 newsletters say that a certain stock will rise, the other 400 say it is going to fall. Again he notes the result and in the third month he sends out newsletter number three to the 400 people who got the correct prediction in the second month. Once again half the newsletters say a certain stock is going to rise, the other half say it is going to fall.

By the fourth month the con man knows that there are 200 people out there who have received three newsletters in a row which have correctly predicted stock prices. The con man now invites these people to pay $500 for an annual subscription. He may even invite them to invest $25 000 in an investment syndicate. Of those 200 people, many will be fooled into thinking that the publisher of the newsletter has a some 'inside knowledge' of the stock market and will eagerly send off their cheques to receive the weekly newsletter. Of course, no newsletter ever arrives: the con man takes the money and disappears. When told of the scam, the victims are amazed to discover that the con man had no knowledge of the stock market at all. After all, did he not correctly 'predict' stock movements three months in a row?

Medical studies have shown that prescribing any medicine, even pills made of sugar, can sometimes bring relief from pain and disease. This effect is called the placebo effect and it comes about because the mind has the capacity to affect the workings of the body and an individual's emotional state has a strong influence on their physical wellbeing. The placebo effect explains why many magical practices seem to be able to cure diseases. It also explains why certain magical practices, such as placing a curse on someone, could actually cause them to fall ill. Such psychosomatic effects (the effect of the mind on the body) convinced people for thousands of years that shamans or witchdoctors possessed genuine powers to heal others or make them sick (which, in a sense, they did possess, since their curses worked, though not for the reasons they maintained).

Religions often use a combination of such statistical and psychosomatic effects. If a charismatic revivalist preacher attempts to 'heal' 1000 people in a year, it is almost certain that some small percentage of them will experience a temporary relief from suffering. It is quite probable that, due to the placebo effect and some incidence of misdiagnosis, some may be permanently 'cured'. If this only occurs to 50 people out of 1000, that is 50 people the preacher can point to as proof of their 'healing power'. Such a number will be enough to make a profound impression on many people even though the success rate (like the stock-market con man) is no better than would have happened anyway.[2]

These of course are intentional scams perpetrated by individuals, usually for money. They illustrate, however, how people can be convinced by what they perceive as the evidence of their own eyes that something is real. If such mechanisms can work in relation to simple physical or medical experiments, the complex and ambiguous fields of economics and sociology provide a rich source of illusory cause-and-effect relationships.

Governments point to economic growth and claim that is the result of their policies—even though it is quite conceivable that the growth may have occurred in any case, and social reformers constantly point out that the 'gap between the rich and poor is widening' although such a widening is the inevitable result of any level of inflation, no matter how small.

The most favourable probabilities are those exploited by water dowsers, or 'diviners', many of whom genuinely believe that they have the power to locate subterranean water for wells. The diviner or 'dowser' wanders around with a stick or another object 'feeling' where there is water under the ground and when the dowser points to a spot, people dig and are usually successful in finding water. The reason that they are usually successful is that there is water under 85 per

---

2   The stock market con man achieves his sample by eliminating the people who receive 'incorrect' newsletters. This also happens with faith healers. Consider people with terminal diseases who go to a faith healer to be cured. If they recover, or go into remission, they form a living testimony that the healing worked, but if they die, they disappear. Thus, like the financial con man, the faith healer's 'errors' are eliminated from the process.

cent of the earth's surface, so the dowser has a better than four out of five chance of being successful, wherever they point. This success rate can be even higher if the dowser has some experience in telling visually where there is more likely to be ground water, for example, away from rocks, or near trees. Despite this, many people still believe that the dowsers have special powers and that they can 'feel' the water through the stick.

In their most pernicious forms, spurious cause-and-effect relationships can be used to mobilise populations to drastic and violent action. The population of Germany in the early part of the 20th century cast around for the 'cause' of their economic problems. National Socialists and other anti-Semites proposed a 'cause' in the form of the Jews who, against all logic, were held to be responsible, simultaneously, for running the financial system *and* the communist movement. The existence of rich Jewish families and Jewish left-wing intellectuals was seen as sufficient 'proof' of the conspiracy: the Jews were the causes of all their problems and had to be removed.

DEFINING 'PROOF'

As I have said, the advent of language introduced the possibility of misinformation to the world. Among the first concepts humans had to learn under this new system were ways of testing the truthfulness of transmitted propositions. Since other humans could not always be trusted it became vital to develop rules that would work as instruments for deciding what was true and what was false. This function was formalised in society by the creation of people who were designated 'judges' and some sense of their importance can be gleaned from the fact that the Book of Judges comes well before the Book of Kings in the Bible. In the folklore of the ancient world the most revered quality was 'wisdom'—the ability to see what was true.

The process of deciding the truth has also been formalised in law, particularly in the rules of evidence, and in the rules of scientific inquiry. However, there are a couple of problems with these systems. The first is that, in the same way as computer viruses become smarter when antivirus programs are introduced and killing bacteria by antibiotics ultimately leads to strains that are resistant to medication, as you establish doctrines to search for invalid doctrines, invalid doctrines become better at evading detection. The other problem is, since the rules for deciding what is true and false are transmitted as doctrines, they themselves must be susceptible to tenetic influences.

Following are some of the common strategies doctrines have evolved to avoid being discredited.

Tenets that cannot be tested

No World Picture can ever be absolutely proved to be true. Our everyday experience tends to continuously confirm theories and models until the day comes when some observation contradicts them. Then the theory or the model has to be changed. However, while theories, models, World Pictures—whatever you want to call them—can never be absolutely proved, they can be disproved. Therefore, what a doctrine must do to survive is guard against being disproved. One way of doing this is to not make assertions that are capable of being discredited.

The magician Uri Geller chose his tricks carefully. It was essentially the low-level nature of his tricks—bending spoons and starting watches—that lent them credibility. Had he chosen to perform tricks such as making the space shuttle disappear, as magician David Copperfield did, it is unlikely that many people would have believed that his powers were real. (Though there would certainly be some.)

Almost any professional magician can perform the sawing-a-lady-in-half trick but it would be a foolish magician indeed who claimed to be able to really saw a woman in half and then rejoin her. If a person claimed to have such powers they would risk being taken to the nearest hospital and asked to use their powers to heal people who had been injured in industrial accidents. When they couldn't do so, their deceit would be quickly revealed. Hence, it is important when claiming supernatural powers, not to make claims which can be directly tested—that is, make sure you keep the doctrine outside the proof zone.

The normal defence against testing used by fakes and charlatans is to say, as Geller always did, that 'the power comes and goes'. This is used by mind-readers, clairvoyants, fortune-tellers and so on to explain why their results are inconsistent (rarely better than chance alone). They postulate that their magical abilities come and go in ways in which they cannot control. Interestingly, their powers always seem to 'go' when they are placed in a position where they cannot use deception.

Religions by and large rely on assertions that are unprovable. Religions win converts by offering rewards to those who adopt the tenets of the faith. The danger of course is that, if the rewards aren't forthcoming, the people will lose faith in the religion. Since it is difficult for a religion to guarantee happiness and success in life, one solution is to claim that the rewards happen in another life. This assertion has the advantage that, while it cannot be substantiated, it cannot be refuted. Since no person has ever returned from a state of death[3] to report on the afterlife, the idea, while it can never be proved, is never disproved and therefore remains intact. The individual either takes the assertion on faith or thinks, 'Well it might be true, why take the risk?'.

The promise of the afterlife is also very effective because human beings fear the idea of death in the absolute sense. That is, beyond the physical experience of dying, the idea of ceasing to exist horrifies them. The idea that consciousness

---

3   Death is probably the furthest from the proof zone you can get.

somehow continues after physical death is therefore very attractive but it is also rather scary. The prospect of an ongoing, eternal life is not very enticing if it is going to be an unpleasant one. Christianity seeks to allay this anxiety by first confirming the idea of eternal life, and then promising that the life will be a pleasant one *if* the person conforms to a fairly simple set of rules. The promise of the reward in the afterlife has traditionally been complemented by a matching promise of hell and damnation for those who disobey the rules. Again, the idea is not supported by one shred of evidence, but it cannot be disproved and this is enough to persuade many people.

Like Christianity, Soviet communism also postulated rewards for citizens after their death. Citizens were told they were working to build a better world that they themselves may never experience, but their children would. The Soviet government also justified some of its disastrous decisions by telling the citizens that the work of the government was beyond their comprehension. It asked them to trust a body of experts supposedly far cleverer than they, who were working for the good of the country. So totally was this accepted that long after the collapse of the Soviet Union in the late 1980s, there were still elderly Russians calling for Stalin's regime to be restored.

Doctrines can also discourage people from trying to test their tenets by warning them of the cost of such experimentation. The people of a primitive tribe may perform a certain ceremony each year before the spring comes in the belief that the ceremony causes the spring to come. Since no one is prepared to risk skipping the ceremony in any year, just in case spring doesn't come and they all die, the irrelevance of the ceremony is never revealed.

Modern populations are still reluctant to experiment with social policies in case their whole society comes tumbling down. Hence, many pointless and sometimes destructive policies and practices prevail because the population is not prepared to take the risk of doing away with them.

Non-specificity

Doctrines are frequently based on tenets that not only cannot be disproved, they cannot even be clearly understood. A very effective defence against being discredited is a proposition so vague that it eludes any attempt to define it precisely. The second of the Ten Commandments states: thou shalt make no graven images. Taken at its face value, this commandment forbids the worship of idols, a feature of many religions of the time. However, it has a more subtle role. It endowed Jehovah with the advantage of having no visual representation, giving the religion the psychological advantage of allowing people to project their own interpretation of the deity. Given the relationship between the monotheistic God and the Internalised Parent, discussed earlier, we can see how this unconscious projection could enhance the emotional power of God. The 'formlessness' of the deity becomes even more important in recent times.

To the earliest humans, the gods—the powerful entities that operated the natural world—were located in the fabric of the earth itself. They resided in the rivers, trees, air and soil. With the coming of the first villages and the first permanent social structures, people updated their concepts of the gods. In Greece and Scandinavia the gods become a circle of heroic characters who lived in their own 'village' on Mount Olympus or in Valhalla. Wider exploration of the world by land and sea, however, failed to find the mystic Olympus, or Valhalla, or Jotunheim, the Islands of the Hesperides or any other mythical locations and the gods began to take on a more spiritual and allegorical nature.

The Hebrews and the early Christians were well placed, or we might say their deity was well placed, in that Heaven was conceived as being physically located above the stars. Here God sat—well out of sight—on a throne surrounded by angels in a real, tangible firmament. This location remained safe from the prying eyes of humans for 1500 years until the growth of astronomy and Galileo's telescope pierced the darkness to reveal not a solid canopy bearing stars, but empty space in which celestial, but not divine, bodies waltzed in time. By the late 19th century, when the universe was starting to be mapped in some detail, the whereabouts of Heaven was becoming a distinct problem for the Church.

One hundred years later, as more and more powerful telescopes look further and further out into infinite space, the possibility of a physical heaven becomes more and more difficult to sustain. The Christian Church's solution over the last 200 years has been to move further towards a mystical and insubstantial view of both God and His abode. By the late 20th century we find theologians referring to Heaven less as physical place, and more as a state of mind, another dimension or state of consciousness, and to God less as a bearded patriarch and more as a primal force, a sort of energy that infuses the universe.

The Church was, wisely, not prepared to relocate God and Heaven to, say, another planet, knowing that the day would come when that too would be explored and found to be devoid of angels. The solution was to shift the whole concept of God and Heaven into a not only unprovable realm but an indefinable one, a realm that by definition could not be accessed by human telescopes, spaceships or logic.

This technique of defining entities as beyond human perception, or beyond human understanding (like the policies of Stalin's government), effectively places concepts beyond scrutiny and therefore beyond the threat of testing and evaluation. The more we examine religious texts and other doctrinal works the more we find that many of the propositions put forward are not real propositions at all. When you try to reduce them down to what we might call 'operational terms' they start to become extremely vague and we see that many of the assertions made are not really assertions at all. Not only are they not testable, they are, like the terms mentioned in the section on language above, not even meaningful. They are empirically unattached words that cannot be associated with any identifiable kind of experience.

Such a lack of direct meaning not only protects tenets from being tested, it allows the tenets to be applied in a very flexible manner. They are not only immune from empirical testing they are protected from accusations of internal inconsistency. For example, if the Christian God is defined primarily as some kind of abstract force that created the universe, then it is not clear how humans can 'talk' to God as if he were a person, or how he has a 'son'. On the other hand, if he is defined as some kind of supernatural but humanoid creature (as he was presumed to be for thousands of years) with a home and a family and feelings that we normally associate with people, then he ceases to be an abstract force and becomes a material being who should be detectable by radar. The solution which evolved was to define God as all or these things—and yet none of them. He is defined as being undefinable, the ultimate defence against intellectual challenge.

Making a virtue of non-provability

Religions and other belief systems frequently protect themselves against logical attack by declaring logic itself to be unreliable or inadequate. It is common for priests to declare the Christian God as being beyond human understanding—a tactic designed to exempt the doctrine from the obligation to make any sense at all.

Thus, when sceptics ask how it is that an all-powerful God who is 'good' causes horrendous things to happen, the answer is forthcoming that 'God moves in mysterious ways'. In other words, when God causes a catastrophe on earth, it is good but in some way that we cannot understand. This answer relies primarily on redefining the word 'good' to include unknown varieties of good of which we are not aware. Since 'good' is, to begin with, a culturally defined term, it is hard for many people to argue with this 'logic'.

The proposition that human logic itself is unreliable is the ultimate lock-out. It protects the doctrine from all criticism based on lack of evidence or reason by maintaining that evidence and reason do not matter. The individual is instructed to suspend the entire reality-testing process and accept the doctrine regardless of any conflict between its tenets and observation or even inconsistencies in the doctrine itself.

Suspension of disbelief can become one of the central tenets of the religion. Accepting the illogical is established as the principal test of entry into the faith, a test which, if passed, will lead to acceptance into the order and eternal life. In other words the doctrine offers a direct and very compelling reward for disobeying logic and reason.

To reinforce this scheme, some doctrines not only offer a reward for suspending disbelief but a system of punishments for those who refuse to do so. Russian intellectuals who dared to question the Communist Party were declared to be 'enemies of the revolution' and were shot. The last thousand years have seen many doubting Christians burned, stoned, hanged and shot as heretics. It is interesting to note that while the rewards for belief were to be received in the next life, punishment for disbelief was felt in *this* one.

The denial of objective reality

The ultimate protection against conflicts with observed reality is a proposition that takes the very concept that our World Pictures are always provisional (true until proven otherwise) and twists it slightly. Denial of objective reality states that if nothing can be shown to be absolutely true then nothing can be shown to be absolutely untrue. In other words, we can believe anything we wish since no belief is any more true than any other one.

This strategy sets out to neutralise the entire principle of reality testing which is to enable the person to make reliable predictions about the world. Of course, no doctrine is

foolhardy enough to maintain that the world is totally subjective, for that would mean that the tenets of the doctrine
are also subjective. The basis of this strategy is to establish
that anything could be true. This allows the doctrine to
blur the distinctions between dream and reality, to allow
the individual to mingle propositions about the outside
world with their own fantasies and wish fulfilment. The
entire effect is not unlike some manifestations of schizo-
phrenia where the individual loses the power to distinguish
between internal imaginings and external realities.

Psychotic as this all sounds, the denial of objective reality
is a central pillar of much postmodern Western philosophy.
These doctrines, borrowing heavily and inaccurately from
Quantum and Relativity Theory in physics, hold that all
reality is 'socially constructed' and that nothing is true in
any objective sense. Superficially, these ideas seem very
similar to ideas propounded in this book. The difference is
the postmodernists cheat. In denying that anything is absolutely true, they make a proposition that purports to be
absolutely true. This leads to the somewhat problematic
tenet:

No proposition is absolutely true.

This is, of course, not what the deconstructivists mean.
What they mean is:

No proposition is absolutely true except this one.

Here we recognise a self-validating statement (that is, it relies
on itself for its own proof). Quite clearly it cannot refer to
any other arguments to prove itself because, according to its
own declaration, all other propositions are unprovable.

In summary, humans test doctrines by comparing their ideas
to the reality they observe around them. However, doctrines
play a major role in both the interpretation of that reality
and formulating the rules that humans apply in making the
comparisons. Many elements that humans think of as 'real'

are actually constructs imposed by doctrines. Furthermore, many of the concepts contained in doctrines—although they purport to reflect some aspect of 'reality'—may be devoid of real meaning, or have meanings that change from moment to moment.

We have seen that doctrines outside the proof zone can persist because they never come into conflict with observed facts, however, doctrines can also influence propositions inside the proof zone by proposing their own rules as to how 'truth' should be decided—rules that essentially protect themselves from being discredited. Such protective techniques involve the invoking of concepts of 'higher logic' or 'the limitations of human logic' or even the denial of objective reality itself.

In other words:

> 25. Doctrines can influence the verification procedures that operate inside the proof zone.

The effect of that influence is that people will accept and perpetuate propositions that have little or no evidence backing them up, or are even meaningless in real terms. This is not to say that all doctrines are anti-empirical but doctrines which are not empirically verifiable can use any and all of the above strategies to attain parity with, or even dominance over, those that are.

CHAPTER 11

DOCTRINES AND INTELLECTUALS

IT MIGHT APPEAR FROM the preceding discussion that when I refer to self-replicating thought systems, I am referring only to religious and political beliefs, but all organised bodies of thought, including academic theories, philosophies, scientific theories, even mathematics, operate according to the same principles. Some, such as scientific theories, have to conform to observed evidence more than others such as philosophy but, as we will see, even scientific theories can circumvent the requirement to produce evidence under certain circumstances.

Because they have positioned themselves as the most credible sector of the community, academics, philosophers and scientists are now more likely to be able to disseminate theories that are regarded as 'true' or 'important' than churches and political parties. Most social observers would agree that over the last century there has been a considerable shift in power from organised religion to the sciences. It is also arguable that, in the late 20th century, that transfer of power continued in the direction of the social sciences. And so we find today that much power, that is to say the power of ideas, which is the real basis of all power in society, lies in the academic world.

DOCTRINES AND EDUCATION

Universities, colleges and research institutions are regarded as the incubators of ideas and academics are regarded as the custodians of intellect and 'truth'; however, it is a serious mistake to think that the principles described in this book do not apply to academics and their institutions as well. In fact, throughout the history of the world, up to and including the present, doctrines have flourished in academic circles more than anywhere else.

The principal concerns of higher education, particularly in the humanities, are theories and models. This also applies to the physical sciences and the social sciences. Students of psychology will be presented with models of human development and cognition formulated by Freud or Piaget just as students of physics will be presented with models of energy propagation created by Maxwell and Dirac.

Traditionally it has been assumed that any theory or model is perpetuated because it fits the observed facts, allows us to make accurate predictions and leads to further testable propositions. However, in accordance with the thesis of this book, a theory may also become popular in academia because:

- it is not disprovable
- it is sufficiently ambiguous as to allow almost any interpretation
- it fits into prevailing fashions of theory construction
- it adds weight to a social or political cause
- it provides opportunities for academic work
- it is associated with individuals or groups that are regarded as powerful
- it refutes opposing theories.

In other words, because it employs tenetic strategies.

As stated earlier in this book, much human knowledge consists of making maps of the environment. Much of our learning also consists of seeing how things are similar to other things. In other words, we create new mental maps of reality by drawing on our existing library of maps. This process can be called making metaphors, analogies, models or diagrams, but it all amounts to the same thing: making something comprehensible by likening it to some existing concept in our brain. We recognise this process, of course, as that most basic of mental functions—generalisation.

Generalisation, as we know, is firstly 'natural'—that is to say it evolved through genetic selection. As we have seen, it is one of the mechanisms by which new ideas are created. However, it is also extremely unreliable. For example, when economists talk about 'pump-priming' in relation to the economy they are not talking about putting water in a metal cylinder with a handle attached. They mean spending a large amount of government money on projects that will provide jobs that will then increase retail sales, that will then increase profits, that will then create more investment, that will lead to more jobs and so on. It is a metaphor which means 'by putting a bit of what we want into a machine, we can make that machine produce more of that substance'. The metaphor is an attempt to make the economy comprehensible to people who don't understand economics but might understand something as simple as a water pump.

The problem with a metaphors such as 'pump-priming', as with other economic metaphors based on plumbing and mechanics, is that they are not accurate. Economic systems do not work on the basis of air pressure forcing a liquid into a pipe, or gravity or momentum or any other physical phenomenon. There is only superficial similarity between the phenomena. The metaphor of the water pump does not really help us understand economics at all and allows us to make no predictions whatsoever regarding the outcomes of government spending during a recession. Human beings, however, because of their inescapable tendency to generalise, are still attracted by models that explain things by likening them to other things we already understand. This is evident in the use of diagrams.

Many theories in both the social and physical sciences, consist first and foremost of diagrams—drawings that conceptualise the theory in the form of shapes, boxes, lines and arrows. This likens often complex material to something we can readily recognise and understand. But there is another reason why diagrams have become popular in theories. Academic theories are propagated almost exclusively in the form of printed papers and books. In other words, to spread your theory abroad, you must find a way to represent complex ideas in a two-dimensional, static, graphic form. Models that look good on the printed page will travel better than models that are messy, wordy or open ended.

The problem with such models is that students reading textbooks in which economic, psychological, social or chemical processes are depicted as diagrams, are likely to think that these visual metaphors depict what the processes are actually like. It is easy to forget that these diagrams and analogies are simply a way of representing the model in a way that can be printed on paper.[1]

Diagrams and visual metaphors are also seen as lending credibility to theories, especially social science theories, because they resemble mechanical systems, which are regarded as being more verifiable. Mechanistic diagrams in psychology and sociology became particularly rife in the early part of the 20th century during a period when engineering and physics were making tremendous advances and were regarded as highly credible disciplines. It was hence quite natural for social scientists to try and emulate engineering

---

1   It is possible to argue that the whole business of representing algebraic concepts in graphs and curves has evolved because mathematics has been disseminated on a planar surface—paper. If you doubt this, consider this question: how might mathematics, its notation and methods and it concepts have evolved over the last 3000 years if the human species was equally intelligent but blind?

with flow charts and diagrams. Of course, the systems that are being described in these models are far more complex than any diagram is usually able to convey, so the theorist ends up adding more and more components until the diagram becomes quite complicated. In the end the simplicity of the model—which was the main reason for devising it—is lost. We cannot help but remember the pre-Copernican cosmologists who had to add so many mechanisms to their earth-centred model of the universe to explain the movement of the planets that the originally elegant model became hopelessly tangled.

This is not, however, necessarily a disadvantage to the doctrine. I have discussed the strategy of making non-provable statements in Chapter 10. We might expect that the world of academic studies would be alert to this technique, and would disregard theories that make untestable propositions, but this is not so. Theories with few or no testable tenets are not uncommon in psychology, economics and, now, even the physical sciences.

Jung's theories of the anima and the animus, the collective unconscious and archetypes; Piaget's theories of schemata; even Freud's theory of the unconscious and the libido are not propositions that can be directly proven. They do not allow us to formulate specific propositions that we can test by experiments or surveys. They are principally a way of organising what we have observed—a way of forming a picture of the mind that gives us the illusion that we actually understand it. As mentioned above, these models usually become quite complex in their attempts to fit all the phenomena they are describing, however this may aid the model since the more complex and abstract that it is, the harder it is to disprove any particular component of it. Thus, Freudian theory is quite capable of stating, without the least sense of embarrassment, that the Oedipus complex can cause a man to be compulsively attracted to women or cause him to be terrified of women. In the same vein some models of global 'warming' predict that the earth will become either warmer or cooler.

In the late 19th and early 20th centuries, research in the social sciences went down two main paths. The first path was that where theorists, encouraged by the spectacular success of applied science and technology, tried to emulate those disciplines in formulating mechanistic models of human society and the human brain. This gave rise to the measurement- and experiment-based work of Psychometrics and the Behaviourists, who believed that only external behaviour could be measured and recorded and the process of 'introspecting' or speculating on one's own mental processes was unscientific. The second path was the path chosen by the psychoanalysts and social psychologists who saw both the mind and society as being based on underlying structures that were largely abstractions drawn from day-to-day observation, anthropological study, even literature and religion.

In 1905 Albert Einstein published his Special Theory of Relativity which, although a theory of physics, was to have a profound effect on academic thought far beyond that field. The Theory of Relativity, together with Max Planck's Quantum Theory, which emerged a few years later, were the first scientific theories since Copernicus to be essentially 'counter-intuitive'; that is to say, they did not merely postulate structures and effects beyond everyday observation, they postulated ideas that appeared to contradict everyday observation. Relativity theory proposed that time slowed down when an object was travelling very fast; Quantum Theory proposed that electrons existed simultaneously as objects and as waves of energy.

Many academics outside the field of physics were not particularly interested in the specifics of these models: what captivated them were the implications for the notions of 'proof' and 'truth'. Einstein's concept that supposedly 'objective' physical events, such as the speed of an object or the measurement of time, could appear different for different observers and Planck's postulate that a particle may have no absolute position or velocity suggested to many researchers (who mostly did not understand either the reasons or the reasoning behind these theories) that the whole idea of objective reality was an illusion. This, combined with widespread disillusionment regarding religious certainties in the late 19th century, appeared to give scientific justification to a number of philosophies that shifted the focus of intellectual activity from searching for 'underlying' truths about God or the universe, to the central problem of living in a world where everything is 'illusory'.

This view of reality as something that was constructed by our cultural and historical perspective was reinforced by the growth of sociology, social psychology and anthropology, which flourished in the early part of the century. It also meshed with the proliferation of political theories that sprang up in the late 19th century. If our view of reality was inculcated by society, then it became arguable that it was inculcated for specific motives. Political reformists and revolutionaries were quick to seize on these concepts to argue that the political, religious and financial power blocs manipulated social perceptions of reality.[2]

The concept was also accepted, and acted upon, by the power blocs themselves who soon began to rely on propaganda machines as much, if not more than, monetary and military coercion to subdue and control populations. Modern capitalism and politics, with their vast expenditure on advertising and media manipulation, still rely on these mechanisms.

This intertwining of scientific, sociological, psychological, political and philosophical thought has led to an interesting situation in modern academic work. Whereas scientific research has become progressively more specialised with very specific theories and hypotheses being tested by highly trained researchers using specially designed tools and

2   A classic example of the 'Sneeze Syndrome' described in Chapter 4. The idea that radical movements program their followers is used by those movements to argue conversely that it is society that programs its members.

methods, research in the social sciences—what are loosely termed 'the humanities'—has become more and more interconnected. It is now almost impossible to envisage any research in the humanities—be it psychological or educational research, analysis of literature, historical study or film criticism—that is not influenced by, and is not required to be influenced by, cultural or political theory.[3]

Thus, we find the academic world dominated by particular philosophical doctrines that have a profound effect on ways of thinking, not just in philosophy itself as a discipline, but in a vast range of other areas as well. It is in fact part of the tenets of these philosophies that all other disciplines must be subordinated to them since they represent an overall view of all intellectual activities. It comes as no surprise when we read advertisements for academic positions that require lecturers in history, literature, film or media to be willing and able to address their subjects from the point of view of gender politics, indigenous politics and identity politics. It is also not surprising to realise that appointment and promotion within colleges and universities also tends to depend on academic staff adhering to certain philosophical and political persuasions.

In these mechanisms we can see many familiar tenetic strategies at work. We see doctrines altering the 'rules' of evidence by marginalising the concept of objective knowledge; the use of non-specific language, which allows theories to be reinterpreted as required; the physical exclusion of dissident academics by making theoretical orientation (as opposed to intellectual skills) a condition of employment; and

---

3   It is interesting to note that the terms 'cultural theories' or 'political theories' have been replaced by the terms 'cultural theory' and 'political theory'. The use of the singular term tends to lend authority to these concepts. Whereas 'theories' has a somewhat tentative feel, 'theory' suggests something real, enduring and integrated. It elevates what is no more than a set of hypotheses to the lofty heights of a whole way of thinking. We might also note that media students do not study 'films' since this suggests they spend their time going to the movies. Instead they study 'film', which invests the topic with an abstract, Platonic quality.

the extensive use of propositions that cannot be disproved. We might also add to this list propositions that cannot be challenged.

PROPOSITIONS YOU CAN'T REFUSE

In Chapter 10 I dealt with propositions that cannot be disproved because there is no way of testing them. But propositions can also resist challenge by erecting emotional barriers to criticism. An example of this would be Marxism, which states that all political theory and action must liberate, ennoble and empower the working class or proletariat. Since the working class was visibly impoverished in the 19th century, any opposition to these tenets could be construed as condoning oppression and advocating social injustice.

Similarly, in the mid-20th century feminist writers exposed the inequalities suffered by women in society. An examination of the causes and remedies of this situation has given rise to far-reaching analyses of society in terms of gender politics. Any attempt, however, to question the validity of a gender-based approach in any given area runs the risk of being labelled 'conservative', 'unreconstructed', 'reactionary', 'sexist' or, most damning of all in academic circles, 'uninformed'. We might also note that, in the latter part of the century, the same emotional protection is afforded to all issues regarding indigenous people. Any attempt to question the beliefs, practices, aspirations or rights of indigenous peoples by members of the dominant culture, is regarded as tantamount to colonial and cultural oppression. Note that all three of these doctrines rely on underlying propositions relating to liberation and social justice that state, as an axiom of social policy, 'thou shalt not oppress'. This axiom is, of course, relatively new in the world and stands as a direct contradiction to the belief, held throughout most of human history, that it is not only beneficial but essential to oppress people in all sorts of ways (see Chapter 5). The fascinating thing about the tenet 'thou shalt not oppress' is that, superficially, it seems to resist the process by which doctrines impose themselves on people—and yet it has been instrumental in spreading many doctrines, including socialism, which have themselves become oppressive. This is another important reminder that, in analysing the effect of a tenet, we must never become distracted by the content of the tenet. What a tenet says and what it does, are vastly different things.

ACADEMIC 'INTELLIGENCE'

In order to propagate, doctrines require human brains that are capable of absorbing and storing complex systems of information. Ironically, this makes people who are capable of incorporating complex ideas into their cortices better candidates for indoctrination than people who have difficulty accommodating such ideas. Put plainly, people who have higher academic intelligence may be more easily programmed than people who have lower academic intelligence. This is perhaps how it came about that some of Hitler's most ruthless executioners were highly qualified academics.

Of course, I am speaking here specifically of academic intelligence. Academic intelligence may be defined as the ability to comprehend (relate to existing constructs in the World Picture) and incorporate (amend the World Picture to match) complex models of reality. This involves an ability with language and ability to deal with 'higher' concepts— concepts built out of, and referring to, other concepts. It is not necessarily the same sort of intelligence as the ability to operate effectively in one's own environment, the ability to perform complex tasks or the ability to independently construct one's own World Picture. Indeed, these abilities may be a hindrance to academic performance.

The academic world is primarily an instrument for the propagation of doctrines presented in the form of theories. Although today we think of universities as being hotbeds of radicalism, they were originally set up in Europe by the

Church as a means of promoting religious doctrines. Despite this historical connection, a non-academic enrolling in a university might reasonably expect to be presented with a usable body of empirical knowledge—and indeed in many disciplines this is the case. In other faculties, however notably psychology, sociology, education, economics, philosophy, history, communications and politics, they are more likely to be presented with theories.

An academic course of study consists primarily of the student reading and hearing about certain theories until they are able to discuss them in detail, compare them and apply them to various real-life situations. What the student is generally *not* expected to do is to question the validity of the theories or even to question why these particular theories should be on the curriculum at all. In an ideal world one would imagine that universities would reward students for questioning and, where appropriate, challenging prevailing theories. In the real world a student who questions those theories is likely to encounter considerable opposition. The simplest reaction is for the academic staff to conclude that the student 'hasn't understood' the theories or given them a fair chance. The student will be dismissed as not being 'qualified' to question the theory because they are not as yet sufficiently versed in it.

Students on the other hand who can converse volubly about the theories and apply the theories—that is to say, express real-life observations in the language of the theory—will be rewarded with high grades and may even go on to become academics in the university or college themselves, whereupon they will commence indoctrinating the next generation of students with the same theories and method.

It is therefore not surprising that the definition of intelligence—in academic circles—has come to be associated with indoctrinability. Abilities such as the capacity to learn skills or to function in the world happily or to create one's own World Picture from available evidence tend to be regarded by academics as lower forms of intelligence. They are likely to be regarded as 'clever', 'interesting', 'intuitive' but 'uninformed'. Note that the term 'informed' does not mean having access to a wide range of empirical information. When academics refer to an individual or a body of work as being 'informed' they mean that the person or their work has been profoundly influenced by some prevailing doctrine.

Just as scholars in the medieval world were taught the prevailing belief systems in relation to God and the Christian cosmos, contemporary scholars are steeped in theories relating to post-industrialised economies, semiology, linguistics, cultural relativism and hundreds of other 'isms' that 'inform' modern education.

DOCTRINES AND PHILOSOPHY

Threatening as it is to suggest that the human mind is running a 'program' like a computer, people have always had some inkling that their thoughts came from 'outside'. In fact, the idea of the human being being under the control of abstract forces was not nearly so threatening before the 20th century. Up until about 100 years ago, the authority of a supreme deity was simply assumed and humans were not regarded as having free will in a complete sense since everything they did and thought was controlled by God (or sometimes the devil—when they were bad). European intellectuals and artists freely acknowledged that their ideas and inspiration came 'from God' because they had a sense of them entering their brains from outside—more or less what tenetics proposes. Isaac Newton, an intensely religious man, described himself as no more than an tool of God, an organ through which God revealed his divine mathematics and physics. Blaise Pascal, another great mathematician, also saw himself as controlled totally by an external, divine force. Thus, humans have for a long time had a sense of not only their behaviour but their thoughts being determined by factors outside themselves. We might even speculate that the idea of the autonomous self, like the autonomous citizen, is a concept born of the industrial age.

Many philosophers have also proposed that ideas have an existence independent of the human mind. From Plato onwards it has been surmised that ideas exist on two planes: an abstract level of pure ideas which existed before the creation of humans and will continue to exist when humans are gone, which only the 'divine being' can truly comprehend; and the everyday level of human ideas that are our crude attempts to understand the pure ideas. What philosophers such as Plato were doing was regarding the general concepts created by the generalisation process as if they were external objects.

Today, we realise that concepts and their labels, words, do not represent divine ideals but are simply mental constructs based on our experiences. As the part of the code of doctrines, words can be reiterated whether or not the person performing the reiteration has decoded the word into meaningful concepts at any stage. Thus, words can become part of the culture whether they have an association with any real-life experience at all. These words may have emotional connotations but they are so vague they defy any attempt to link them directly to any observed experience. There is no doubt, for example, that terms such as 'right' and 'wrong' evolved as tools for naming real actions and real situations— their purpose was quite practical—and they are still used in this way, to denote something that is correct or incorrect according to clearly defined criteria. However, because words and concepts came to be regarded as our inadequate attempts to grasp ideals that existed on the abstract plane, much philosophical energy has gone into trying to work out the nature of 'absolute good' and 'absolute evil'. Few philosophers in the 20th century regarded concepts such as 'right' and 'wrong' as having any existence outside the culture in which they are employed but for previous generations of philosophers, ideas were real things and their job was to discover the nature of them.

Philosophers therefore have spent centuries trying to find ways of proving the existence of things, such as 'goodness', which cannot be proved. Not surprisingly, they often concluded that these things cannot be proved. However, this has led to the further conclusion not that these things should be regarded as having no objective existence, but that their objective existence had to be accepted as *self-proving*. In other words, one had to accept that there were some things for which no proof was required. We recognise this, of course, as one of the most common survival strategies employed by doctrines—denying the necessity of proof.

Thus, philosophers have spent thousands of years chasing their tails, seeking ways to prove the existence and meaning of absolute concepts that have no real existence, and then, finding that such proof is not possible, seeking ways to prove why proof is not possible or necessary. What we see here is the dilemma of the human mind, which naturally tries to form a consistent picture of the world, struggling to deal with the illogicalities and inconsistencies of the doctrines that dominate its World Picture, but having only the language, meanings and rules of logic of the doctrines themselves with which to do so. The result is a tremendous confusion as the mind tries to use the tenets of the doctrine to test the doctrine—an almost impossible feat since doctrines rarely include tenets that enable their own interrogation. On the contrary, most doctrines have evolved tenets specifically designed to protect themselves from examination and discreditation.

The result of trying to perform this impossible feat, trying to verify doctrines that are not verifiable, is a kind of mental derangement. The writings of many philosophers are indistinguishable from the writings of schizophrenics, people who are suffering from thought disorder. The analogy is not frivolous since one of the central dysfunctions of the schizophrenic is that the sufferer loses the ability to distinguish between imagination and reality. In the same way, philosophers, in trying to find a logical structure in a doctrine such as Christianity where there is no such structure, leave the real world and become lost in a swamp of transcendental, intangible, unprovable, indefinable concepts until they sink in the intellectual quicksand. They are essentially tragic figures, the victims of doctrines, intelligent and articulate people who have ultimately resorted to a kind of highly intellectualised insanity in an attempt to justify the tenets of self-replicating thought systems.

If we revert to thinking about ideas as programs we see that systems of logic are programs that sort propositions into true and untrue piles. Unfortunately, it is not too hard to come up with propositions that will throw the testing process into a loop, for example, if we feed in the statement 'this statement is not true'. This is a proposition that makes a statement about itself. The problem is, if what the statement says is true, then the statement is not true. On the other hand, if the statement is not true, then it must be true. This is what is traditionally called a paradox but is really just a loop in a truth-testing program. It is the same as two instructions in a computer program that say:

Instruction 998   Go to Instruction 345
Instruction 345   Got to Instruction 998

Bertrand Russell, the mathematician and philosopher, proposed a problem with the 'set of all sets which include themselves'. An example of a 'set which includes itself' would be the set of all things that are not screwdrivers. A set is not a screwdriver and so it is a member of the group—in other words, it is a member of *itself*. Russell's problem arose when he considered the set of all sets that do *not* include themselves, such as the set of armadillos. A set is not an armadillo and so the set of armadillos is not a member of itself. The 'set of all sets that do *not* include themselves' includes the set of screwdrivers, the set of armadillos, the set of shoes, and so on virtually to infinity. The problem was, was this set a member of itself?

If the set was a member of the set that meant it was a set which included itself, but it *can't* be a member of the set because it was supposed to be the set of sets which *didn't* include themselves. On the other hand if the set was *not* a member of the set, then it *was* a member of the set because this was supposed to be the set of sets which were not members of themselves.

Confused? Russell was so perturbed by his inability to find a logical solution to the paradox that his whole faith in mathematics was shaken to the core, and he never again applied himself to mathematics and logic with the same enthusiasm.

Of course, there is no such thing in reality as 'the set of all sets that are not members of themselves'. It is an artefact of syntax just like the sentence, 'This sentence is not true'. They are simply collections of words that send a logic program spinning in a loop. The amazing thing is that philosophers still attempt to solve such paradoxes and feel distressed when they cannot. They feel that there should be a solution, but they can't find it because they are still running the program. They cannot break the loop because they continue to see the rules of logic that they are trying to apply as real things not just programs running in their brains. In other words, in some ways we have not progressed past Plato. At the same time, philosophers often convey an intuitive sense—albeit an unconscious one—that programs or doctrines are constraining their thinking. Jean Jacques Rousseau, for example, argued in 1755 that science, art and social institutions had corrupted mankind and that people should try and revert to a natural state, which he saw as the only 'pure' state of being, untainted by transmitted culture.[4]

The philosopher Georg Wilhelm Friedrich Hegel introduced the idea of 'dialectics'—opposing ideas which strive for dominance in the abstract world. This is extremely close to the tenetic idea of doctrines battling for dominance of the External Memory and the individual mind. Hegel, of course,

---

4   Like many other philosophers, in his later years Rousseau contradicted his earlier writings and advocated strict obedience to social laws.

had no understanding of the modern concept of programming and so saw these dialectics as emanations of eternal abstract ideas. All the same, his sense of the struggle anticipates the model of thinking outlined here.

The Austrian-born philosopher Ludwig Wittgenstein argued in 1921 in his book *Philosophical Investigations* that 'philosophy is a battle against the bewitchment of our intelligence by means of language', a statement that anticipates some of the contentions of this book. He said the resolution of philosophical problems must entail an analysis of the different 'games' involved in using language. We can view this idea as being closely related to the tenetic concept of language as a strategic tool of doctrines.

Marx took Hegel's idea of a contest between dialectics and adapted it to the conflict between social, political and, in particular, economic systems. However, to rid dialectics of its idealist and religious element, Marx grounded his dialectics in what was called a materialist foundation. This allowed Marx to present his theory of historical materialism—that social history is the history of production of goods—as if it were a scientifically based theory. The interesting feature of Marx's historical materialism is that it was deterministic: it pronounced that capitalism would *inevitably* die and be replaced by a more advanced system.

Determinism is, put simply, the concept that since every event is the result of a preceding event, the flow of history is predestined or fixed. It gives rise to the idea that if we could know the entire state of the universe at any given moment we could theoretically predict its state one second later. By repeating the process we could therefore predict the entire course of the future. What this suggests is that the history of the universe was determined at the outset and the future is already fixed (though we don't know what it is) and that history could not have been other than it was.

Determinism directly contradicts the idea of free will, which holds that people make choices. Determinism states that people have no real choice: the outcome of their decisions has already been decided in advance. The determinism versus free will debate has been central to philosophy since the beginning of civilisation and has been a problem for religions such as Christianity, which holds that God controls every event in the universe while at the same time claiming that humans are free to make choices. These two tenets are often identified as being mutually exclusive and 'heretics' have asked why, for example, humans should be thrown into Hell for committing sins when, if God controls everything, He has caused them to commit the sin in the first place. The idea seems to represent sheer victimisation by the deity.

Marxism, which firmly rejected all religion, came down firmly on the side of determinism, arguing that the world was inevitably headed for a socialist future. The problem was that Marx had really just borrowed the term 'determinism', as he borrowed the term 'dialectic', to lend credibility to his revolutionary theories. In fact, it was not a theory of determinism at all but a mixture of wishful thinking and a blatant attempt to create a self-fulfilling prophecy.

Nevertheless, the growth of scientific inquiry in the 19th and 20th centuries has led to a greater reliance on the concept of determinism. Tenetics is itself a deterministic model. It suggests, as outlined in Chapter 3, that human behaviour will depend on a particular neuron firing and that in turn will depend on the net effect of the multipliers and inhibitors operating at any given moment. In the same chapter we saw the proposition that doctrines cause humans to enact certain behaviours (that is, cause certain neural outcomes) by activating emotional states that favour particular responses. We also saw that doctrines combine in the human brain to produce what are perceived to be new and original ideas. The tenetic view of free will is that it is an illusion, though a very convincing one. The human being is aware of drives and emotions competing in their brain— a feeling of 'having to make a decision'. They are also aware of the doctrines that exist in, and compete for, control of their World Picture—the sense of 'considering the issues'.

They will also be aware of 'making a decision', which is the point where their mind resolves the inconsistency (what psychologists call 'cognitive dissonance') and a particular action is performed, or a particular tenet is elevated to the status of 'true' within the World Picture. The making of the choice is usually accompanied by a feeling of relief as the tension arising from the competition between ideas and feelings dissipates.

Twentieth-century philosophers have reacted variously to the implications of determinism, sometimes arguing for and against the concept simultaneously (as theologians did for a thousand years before them). Sören Kierkegaard, the founder of the somewhat diverse Existentialist movement, reacted against Hegel's concept of abstract ideals and stressed the necessity of the individual formulating their own beliefs—though it was his intention that their belief would ultimately be in God. His famous follower Jean-Paul Sartre also condemned determinism as exonerating people from taking responsibility for their own actions. He asserted that individuals must take responsibility for their actions without relying on traditional beliefs of religious teachings. Later in life however, Sartre swung more towards the Marxist view that people are socially conditioned by historical forces. Sartre believed that there was a loss of 'self' in the modern world that could only be remedied by collective, revolutionary, action—a seeming acknowledgment that the power of doctrines could only be met by the power of an equal and opposite doctrine.

Martin Heidegger, another philosopher of the Existentialist school, wrote that cultural objects, including concepts as well as material objects, came from the past but were used by people for dealing with the present and the future—an idea obviously related to the idea of transmitted knowledge and constructed reality. Heidegger felt that the individual was in danger of being 'submerged' in the external world and losing their sense of free will and autonomy. Heidegger's theory was that this loss of 'authenticity' in the individual, that is the feeling that their thoughts and actions were not their own, led to a sense of Angst or fear. The only remedy for Angst was to engage in an active confrontation with external culture and reality. We might opportunistically equate this to saying that people need to get back to empirical selection (described in Chapter 8). Thus, philosophers from Rousseau to Heidegger reflect a tension between personally acquired knowledge and socially imposed knowledge in regard to forming a sense of self.

This idea of the sense of self being created by society was combined with Marxist theory by Michel Foucault to form a view that our concept of self was the product of existing power blocs in society. Foucault identified a form of power called bio-power whereby philosophies harness the energy of biological systems, a concept obviously similar to the idea of activation. He also questioned the idea of authorship, as I did in Chapter 8, seeing that, in many ways, authors merely channelled existing concepts into new configurations.

Foucault addressed the ways in which ideas and perceptions of truth changed over time, using terms such as rupture, break, gap, displacement, mutation, shift, interruption and lacuna to describe successive shifts in power between ideas. He and other 20th century philosophers speak of the genealogy of philosophical thought, implying an evolutionary tree of theory, similar to the evolutionary tree of biological species. However, what few of the postmodernist philosophers and their predecessors did was ask why their particular philosophy appeared at the time it did.

The assumption made by philosophers is that their theories represent a necessary advance in human thinking and that their philosophy is in some sense right for its times. The possibility that their theories gratify some immediate popular need in society is rarely considered. For example, in the second half of the 19th century when the cities of Europe were teeming with low-paid industrial workers, it is scarcely surprising that a philosophy that predicts that the class system would give way to an egalitarian society, gained popularity. We might ask how successful a political philosophy that predicted the perpetual slavery of the working class would have been. In the 20th century when unprecedented numbers of middle-class children, beneficiaries of free compulsory education systems in the Western democracies, started to attend universities, is it any wonder that philosophies that advocated a questioning of traditional authority and the overthrow of entrenched power structures were popular with students and teachers who wanted to be popular with students?

Philosophical theories, however (with the exception of Marxism with its tenets relating to historical determinism), generally do not attempt to account for their own presence in the world nor do they acknowledge the tenetic strategies that are included within their own principles. A typical philosopher does not begin the preface to their book with the sentence, 'I have deliberately designed the elements of this theory to ensure that it will appeal to middle-class academics working in US universities where it will create enough interest to spawn hundreds of academic papers and maybe even my own magazine and research institute—at the very least a professorship for me at Yale'.

Rather, philosophers write with the utmost earnestness, positioning their theory as a set of 'true' statements which promise enlightenment and empowerment for the individual and an all-round better world, while at the same time employing all the tricks described above—non-specific terms, untestable propositions, idiosyncratic rules of evidence, the creation of a private language that requires a 'priesthood' to interpret it—even the denial of objective reality—to give their theory a competitive edge in the philosophical marketplace.

Tenetics is related to philosophy in two ways. First, as outlined earlier, we can see that philosophy and philosophers throughout the ages have attempted to deal with the same issues that tenetics does though they have used different language and started from different assumptions. At the same time, tenetics holds that philosophies are social artefacts just like rock 'n' roll music, comics, insurance and astrology and thus legitimate fields for tenetic analysis. In other words, we can examine a philosophy from two totally different points of view. We can examine the validity of the theory as a system of thinking—analyse its tenets and decide whether we think they are true, useful or meaningful to us. We can discuss whether they help us understand ourselves or the world, or cast any light on other theories. Conversely, we can look at the theory as a social phenomenon and ask, 'How does it attract people? How does it reproduce itself? How does it deal with criticism? How does it compete with other phil-osophies?'. The second approach, the approach I have used in this book, seeks to analyse philosophies as psychological and sociological processes. It does not offer a critique of the theory as a logical system.

It comes as no surprise that philosophers tend to encour-age the former approach rather than the latter. For example, here is part of an introduction to *The Basic Problems of Phenomenology* by Martin Heidegger:

> . . . our purpose is not to acquire historical knowledge about the modern movement in philosophy called phenom-enology. We shall be dealing not with phenomenology but with what phenomenology itself deals with. And, again, we do not wish merely to take note of it so as to be able to report then that phenomenology deals with this or that subject; instead, the course deals with the subject itself, and you yourself are supposed to deal with it, or learn how to do so, as the course proceeds. The point is not to gain some knowledge about philosophy but to be able to philosophise.

Heidegger is telling prospective philosophy students that the purpose of the course is not to study the philosophy objectively as a phenomenon but to begin to think about the world according to the philosophy, to adopt the methods of the philosophy and start to think according to its tenets. In fact, philosophy itself, as an area of intellectual endeavour, is a system of doctrines that, like the religions out of which they have grown and to which they are still strongly linked, have created their own presence in the world.

Today, philosophy has less to do with logical rigour than it has to do with how academics are promoted and have their works published. It is not the purpose of this book to go into the conditions that have shaped the nature of philosophical doctrines over the last hundred years except to say that philosophy in the 20th century has demonstrated all the survival strategies employed by doctrines: denial of objective proof, harnessing of emotional energies and intimidation of opponents. Some philosophers have even espoused violence as a legitimate means of enforcing their tenets.

DOCTRINES AND SCIENCE

Philosophers, and philosophical theories generally, tend to suggest that philosophy is a prerequisite for science—that philosophy acts as an epistemological guide for science, checking its directions, its methods and its validity. To quote Martin Heidegger:

> In the early period of ancient thought philosophia means the same as science in general. Later, individual philosophies, that is to say, individual sciences—medicine, for instance, and mathematics—become detached from philosophy. The term philosophia then refers to a science which underlies and encompasses all the other particular sciences. Philosophy becomes science pure and simple. More and more it takes itself to be the first and highest science or, as it was called during the period of German idealism, absolute science.

This kind of statement is common from philosophers though it is, significantly, less common from scientists. The reality is that science is capable of functioning perfectly well without any input from philosophy at all. Why? Because science is no more than a concentrated form of everyday human thinking. It differs in its complexity, its thoroughness, its rigour, but not in its method or the types of questions it asks.

Scientific investigation is essentially an extension of how people faced with a problem go about solving that problem in a methodical manner. Thus, people who have no acquaintance with any European philosophical theories at all, be they Amazonian Indians, Berber nomads, carpenters in Birmingham or chemists in Geneva are all capable of conducting their business and generating perfectly valid working knowledge which allows them to master their world. Furthermore, science purely and simply seeks to find meaningful answers to meaningful questions, whereas philosophy can occupy itself extensively with questions that have no meaningful interpretation at all. Thus, rather than being an aid, philosophical doctrines may represent a danger to the natural process of discovery which science embodies.

Because of the contamination of philosophy by doctrines, such as religion, from the 19th century onwards thinkers have turned to science to provide some measure of objectivity in their picture of the world. In the 20th century, however, science too has become alarmingly doctrinal.

Throughout the 19th century many remarkable advances were made in scientific knowledge and theoretical modelling. James Clerk Maxwell reconciled the equations for electricity and magnetism, the mechanism of radio-active decay was identified, and the structure of the atom was observed by Ernest Rutherford. Of all the scientific announcements of the era, the ones with the greatest implications for the wider world were those made in 1905 by Albert Einstein in his Special Theory of Relativity.

As I have mentioned before, Einstein's purpose was to devise a model for physics that could incorporate several contradictory observations that had been made, mostly involving the speed of light. Einstein postulated a model of the universe in which these observed events 'made sense'. The problem was the model itself challenged conventional views of reality. It suggested, among other things, that time slowed down when an object was moving fast compared to another and that gravity could 'bend' space–time. The theory caused

storms of controversy for years and is still not totally accepted although many of Einstein's 'predictions' (the tenets of
his model) have since been found to match the results of
experiments and observations.

The Theory of Relativity was a watershed for science,
not merely because it challenged Isaac Newton's classical
model of the universe in which time and space were laid out
in nice straight lines. It was revolutionary because it involved
no experimental work by Einstein at all: it was purely a
thought exercise. The experiments that subsequently confirmed some of its tenets were not even dreamed of at the
time the theory was formulated. It is true that Einstein set
out to reconcile the results of other people's experiments
but his theory was not in itself an experimental or observational work. It was purely an exercise in constructing an
abstract model of the universe that would conform to the
observations made in earlier experiments.

At the same time other scientists were making equally
baffling pronouncements about the structure of matter at
the sub-atomic level. Particles, declared some theorists, were
sometimes in two or more places at the same time. Again,
these models were an attempt to reconcile experimental
results that suggested that particles were simultaneously like
a wave passing through a medium and a discrete object
moving through space. These theories were also furiously
attacked by classical physicists who refused to allow a notion
as fundamental as the whereabouts of an object to be aban-
doned. In the true spirit of all doctrinal debate, one of the
most vehement opponents of these new 'quantum' theories
of matter was none other than Einstein who, while he could
accept a concept as paradoxical as the curvature of space,
could not accept the notion of 'superposition' (a particle
being in two places at once) in Quantum Theory.

Einstein continued to adapt his theory to include Maxwell's
equations of electromagnetism in the General Theory of
Relativity, which he published in 1916. Since that time others
have reconciled Relativity with Quantum Theory and many

physicists are still trying to incorporate the concept of gravity into Einstein's model, a problem he wrestled with for the remainder of his life.

The Theory of Relativity eventually helped solve a number of problems in particle physics and cosmology. The problem with the theory was that in attempting to forge a model that would incorporate all known experimental results and all known theories, it fostered the idea that developing and perfecting such a model—a Grand Unified Theory (G.U.T.) or Theory of Everything (T.O.E.)—was the primary goal of science. For the remainder of the 20th century physicists—or least physicists who have taken to writing popular books about physics—promoted the idea of one great overarching theory as the ultimate goal and end of science (as some writers have literally put it), ignoring the fundamental problem that even if such a model could be formulated we could never know if it was the only possible one.

No matter how comprehensive the model was and no matter how completely it was verified by experimental and observational data, we could never conclude that the model was complete or perfect, because there would always be the possibility that some event could occur that would shatter the model overnight. And yet, scientists in the late 20th century focussed on the Theory of Everything as if its discovery were just around the corner and it was about to provide the final answer.

How did science manage to lose sight of one of its most important principles? In considering this, it is worth noting that the Theory of Relativity and Quantum Theory were generated about the time when scientists reached the limits of observation. Einstein was dealing with models of the universe that were beyond the capacity of his contemporaries to see or measure. Planck and the other Quantum theorists were dealing with a realm that could not be directly observed because it was smaller than the wavelength of light and therefore invisible. In other words, early in the 20th century, as far as the experience of the ordinary person goes, physics moved out of the proof zone.

Most of us don't have a problem with Newtonian physics because we see (and feel) the principles of gravity, inertia, and action and reaction every day when we drive cars, throw balls or open doors. However, most us rarely travel at three quarters the speed of light and so cannot personally verify the phenomena that Einstein's theory predicts.

Since that time our observational capacities have been greatly extended, enlarging the proof zone, at least for some people. Radio telescopes and space telescopes have extended our visual reach and more and more powerful cyclotrons, synchrotrons and supercolliders have generated the immense energies required to smash sub-atomic particles into their constituent parts. However, inspired by the 'grail' of the G.U.T., this new information has prompted physicists to hurtle even further into the unknown, producing a plethora of cosmological models including 11 or 23 dimensional universes, string theories, superstring theories, inflationary bubbles of space and, of course, the ever popular Big Bang.

These theories have been accompanied by a corresponding spate of books, papers and television programs written by, and about, theoretical physicists, some of whom have become media personalities, explaining the tenets of the Big Bang and other theories and looking forward to the forthcoming T.O.E. or G.U.T., which will provide one set of equations to explain the entire existence of the universe and everything in it.

What is unfortunately omitted in these books that line the shelves of bookstores are intellectual health warnings that theories such as the Big Bang or 11-dimensional space are no more than models that have been generated to explain the phenomena of the universe as we currently experience them. Many of these models, including the Big Bang, violate many of the principles that define proper empirical method. They:

- include non-testable propositions
- are not amenable to controlled experiment or observation

- introduce extraordinary factors to avoid inconsistencies with more established theories. For example, certain versions of the Big Bang theory contradict relativity by suggesting that the universe expanded faster than the speed of light. The contradiction is resolved by arguing that matter did not actually move through space faster than light but that space itself expanded. The paradox that this creates is ignored.

These models are constantly described in various publications and television documentaries as if they were proven facts when they are in fact models and all models are provisional.

But how do members of the public verify the physicists' work? The success of most scientific theories lies in the fact that, once they are communicated to the public and the public overcomes the shock of the paradigm shift, the theories start to look self-evident. So, while it is unlikely that a non-astronomer might have proposed the Copernican model of the solar system, the model, once accepted, seems to be vindicated by everyday experience: the alternation of night and day, the movement of the stars across the sky and the change of seasons. It all makes sense. But a model of 11-dimensional space can never be confirmed by ordinary experience—at least not mine. Similarly, the long and complicated mathematical proofs on which many of these models are based are solely the domain of specialised mathematicians. The rest of us have to take their word for it.

It is of course worth remembering that the mathematical definition of 'proof' is quite different from the conventional definition of proof. Mathematical proof means that an expression can be derived from another expression by the application of certain rules. How do we know that the rules are valid? The answer is that they are proved by more basic rules and those rules are proved by even more basic rules. Thus, the house of mathematics is built of sets of rules, piled on top of each other, each set supporting the set above it.

Does this mean that the results of mathematical reasoning represent truths about the real world? Certainly not. The results of mathematical logic are only true or untrue in relation to the system of mathematics. While they may mirror or suggest some condition of the real universe they cannot prove any such condition. It must be confirmed independently by observation: nothing can be proved by deduction alone.

Mathematicians, of course, regard mathematics as a pure form of reasoning which transcends the prejudices and weakness of human minds—a concept reminiscent of the Platonic belief in ideal concepts that reside on the supernatural plane—and maintain that, providing the rules are applied correctly, mathematical reasoning constitutes a form of absolute and irrefutable logic. However, like philosophy—with its anomalies such as Russell's paradox—mathematics is perfectly capable of following its impeccable logic to arrive at absurd conclusions. Georg Cantor, a 19th century mathematician, was able to 'prove' mathematically that there are different classes of infinity, some bigger than others— a finding which violates the definition of the term. Kurt Gödel, the author of the famous 'incompleteness theorem', claimed, towards the end of his life, to have discovered a mathematical proof for the existence of God.

What we must bear in mind constantly is that mathematics, like all systems of thought, is a doctrine that brings with it its own definitions of proof and truth. Its propositions, expressed in symbolic form like language can only be, at their very best, a representation of reality, not reality itself. Nor are they an exact or complete representation. The ratio of a circle to its diameter (π) has been caclulated to over a million decimal places but still cannot be expressed as an exact fraction of a number even though it is a fundamental property of our universe. Conversely, many mathematical entities such as the square root of minus one do not occur in the real world (although some equations containing $\sqrt{-1}$ model the behaviour of chaotic systems such as air turbulence).

The problem with mathematics is that, because it has become so specialised in the 20th century, it is increasingly difficult to place its tenets (its methods) under any widespread scrutiny. Any attempt by a layperson to suggest that perhaps mathematics does not reflect reality is instantly discredited by mathematicians who declare—much like academics when they are defending their philosophical and political theories—'But they don't understand the maths'. This is recognisable as a shell strategy where the doctrine is preserved by a carefully educated priesthood that maintains the flame and protects the concepts from challenge by the outside world.

This is not to say that mathematics does not 'work' in the real world. A vast number (though by no means all) of our technological achievements are the result of, and stand as validations of, mathematical calculation and reasoning. But mathematics, like any sort of computation program, is only as reliable as the data that is fed into it. It cannot evaluate the validity of its starting points, nor can it tell if its results contradict empirical evidence. It is only a tool and a dumb tool at that, though from time to time it has the capacity to reveal something as unexpected as the Mandelbrot Set.[5]

Despite these limitations, many contemporary scientific models of cosmology and particle physics rely almost wholly on mathematical reasoning. The net effect is that many areas of science have now become as removed from traditional scientific method as philosophy has become removed from logic and again we are faced with the problem of what to do when the instruments we have put in place to guard us against doctrines become susceptible to doctrinal influences.

---

5   Putting a particular mathematical expression into a computer program and asking it to perform repeated calculations based on the expression gives rise to a startling pattern called the Mandelbrot Set, which has amazing properties. The most interesting of these is that you can magnify it infinitely and it will still display the same types of patterns.

CHAPTER 12

HOW DO WE KNOW WHAT IS TRUE?

I F OUR PERCEPTION OF the world is constructed by doctrines, we might ask the questions: 'Is everything illusion? Is there no objective truth? Can we ever think independently?'. Fortunately, we do still have mechanisms that offer some hope of transcending the constructs implanted in us by doctrines.

SCIENCE

Science, in its purest form, is a method by which a World Picture is constructed and verified by the application of certain rules of evidence. Courts, where people's lives hang in the balance, also employ rules of evidence to try and guarantee some measure of justice to the accused, plaintiff, respondent or victim.

Stated simply, the empirical method requires the following:

1. All propositions must be testable. A proposition that cannot be tested is essentially useless because we can never tell whether it is true or false. It is therefore simply unnecessary baggage in our view of the world. It may be true, it may be false. We can never know.

2. A proposition can only form part of our World Picture if it is supported by evidence that is the result of controlled observation and controlled experiment. There are a number of rules that define what a controlled observation or experiment is. They are designed to ensure that misleading results are not obtained or, even when the results are accurate, misleading conclusions are not drawn from them.

3. Propositions in our World Picture must be consistent with each other. We cannot, for example, simultaneously believe that:
   (a) The elasmosaurus lived in very warm climates.
   (b) The elasmosaurus lived in the Permian age.
   (c) The earth was very cool during the Permian age.
   One (or more) of these propositions will have to be modified before the whole set can be accepted in our World Picture.

4. No general rule is ever absolutely proved except by definition, for example, 'all triangles have three sides'. By definition a polygon that has three sides is a triangle. By definition no numerical or quantitative value can ever be assigned to infinity. The ultimate safeguard of the empirical method is that evidence can only confirm a belief, it can never prove it absolutely. Experiment and observation can disprove a proposition and prove a specific or limited instance of a proposition ('my dog has legs' or 'all the dogs in this room have legs') but we cannot absolutely prove a general proposition ('all dogs have legs') no matter how many dogs we observe.

These rules lead us to recognise several things about the empirical World Picture:

- Our models of reality are always works in progress. We must be constantly testing and refining our beliefs and looking for inconsistencies and flaws. Every new piece of data slightly affects the existing model and all the elements of the total picture. New information is constantly added to the model and must be reconciled with all the existing precepts. This is not to say that we never know anything for sure—after all, some propositions are being continually confirmed to the extent that we can place a high degree of confidence in them. ('If I put my hand on the hotplate when it is switched on it will hurt.') There is no reason to become paralysed by a sense that 'nothing is real'. All we must remember is that what we have always taken to be true may turn out to be not 100 per cent accurate.

- We must learn about testing procedures and particularly be aware of mechanisms that produce false results or false conclusions such as invalid experiments, invalid statistics and invalid logic. The price of liberty, it is said, is eternal vigilance. The same might be said of our models of reality. Every piece of data must be scrutinised with the awareness that the world is dominated by doctrines, and part of the operation of doctrines is to distort data and distort interpretation. When in doubt we should always institute our own investigations, run our own experiments, do our own research or be satisfied that the sources of our information are not contaminated by doctrines.

- We must be constantly alert for untestable propositions masquerading as theories.

- We should never be persuaded to any belief simply because it is supported by a large number of people or a large body of literature. It is always worth remembering that, at every point in history 90 per cent of what was regarded as 'true' has later on been shown to be in some sense 'untrue' and we must assume that the same is probably true of the times in which we live.

- We should not become too intent on formulating grand models for the universe, especially since such models are mostly nothing more than inaccurate generalisations from other phenomena. Instead, we should concentrate on finding out what 'works' by empirical selection. In other words, while we might never know what the universe is like, we can still know what the universe 'likes'. We may never be absolutely certain as to why something works but as long as we are sure that it does work we can be sure that our knowledge is being shaped by the underlying laws of the cosmos.

• No person should ever feel that they are not qualified to question the prevailing wisdom of the times. The notion that the commonsense of ordinary people and their observations of the world are inferior to the intelligence and knowledge of the educated and the expert is simply one of the myths promoted by doctrines to maintain their domination of the human species.

Persons who maintain these principles are known as sceptics ('skeptikos' for those who prefer the original Greek spelling) a term often taken to mean people who refuse to believe in anything. It would be more correct to define modern sceptics as people who refuse to believe in anything until it has been proven to some reasonable standard.

Computer users will be familiar with the concept of a 'rescue disk', a disk that is formatted when you install an anti-virus program on your computer. Since you cannot clean a virus from your computer while it is running a virus-infected program, many virus protection programs set up a 'clean boot disk', which you can keep in a drawer for emergencies. If you suspect your machine has a virus, you start up the computer from the clean floppy disk and then search your computer's internal disks for infection.

In a sense, sceptics are the 'rescue disks' of society. They are there when everyone else is infected with a doctrine to question that doctrine and see that it is subjected to proper testing procedures. Traditionally, science has been seen as having this role but even science is prone to exploitation by doctrines and must be continually subjected to rigorous scrutiny. But it is worth mentioning another human activity that also provides us with an insight into what is 'real', and that, surprisingly for some, is art.

ART

As we have seen, the existence of doctrines is the result of humans' ability to codify their thoughts and experiences as language and pass them on to others. The critical issue here is 'codify'. Each human has a unique life and the record of this life results in a unique record of experience stored in the brain as neural connections. The question is, how can a unique set of experiences be communicated by language which must, for reasons of practicality, be shared by the whole community and limited to a few thousand words? Inevitably, some simplification of the experience must occur. This presents us with two communications problems.

1. The knowledge we receive is knowledge that has been simplified to enable it to be transmitted through language.
2. When we try to communicate our thoughts and feelings, we must simplify them in order to code them into language.

In other words while we use 'dog' to refer to a (dog) or even [dog], the *word* 'dog' is not the same thing as the *concept* of [dog] or the actual *experience* of a (dog). The word cannot cause the experience, it can only evoke the listener's concept of [dog], which is in turn derived from their memories of (dogs).

We encounter these problems in, for example, writing about or reading about a historical event. In describing a war, it is not possible to translate every event, thought and feeling experienced by everyone who was involved in the war so the writer has to be selective. They may decide to concentrate on the decisions of the commanders, they may decide to follow the story of one particular platoon, they may focus on the experiences of one particular soldier. Whatever the choice, the writer selects one line of information out of all the possible information available and records it for transmission. Eventually, if no one else records it, that other information is lost.

Anything about real events that is communicated to us by symbolic language has suffered information loss. Similarly, when we record or communicate the events, thoughts and feelings of our own lives, we are also somewhat hampered. If we are one of the soldiers in the war, we can describe the events in terms of where we were and what we did. However, if we wish to convey the experience itself as it occurred to us, including our emotions, we may have some difficulty finding words to express that information with any sort of completeness. When one person describes an experience to another, they are essentially trying to put the other person's nervous system into the same state that their own is in, or was in at the time of the event. Of course, creating a complete copy of that state is impossible. We may say we were 'frightened' or 'sad' and these terms may signify certain emotional states to the listener but they do not convey the actual experience of those feelings. Words, to use an electronics term, are 'lossy'—information is lost in transit.

In order to better transmit the thoughts, feelings and experiences—all the structures in our cerebral cortex—that symbolic propositions cannot code, humans have developed art. The first technique of art to emerge was mimesis, or imitation. Here, the work of art attempts to convey experiences directly to the audience by creating objects and events that perceptually resemble aspects of the original experience. In other words, mimetic art uses an analog coding mechanism—the work in some way resembles what it represents. A hunter–gatherer draws the outline of a bison on the wall of a cave. Rather than describing a mountain range in words, a painter reproduces her own perceptions of its colours, lustre and texture in oils on canvas. A sculptor reproduces the torso of his lover in marble. Actors on a stage simulate interactions between people to convey subtleties of behaviour and emotion that a psychology textbook cannot convey. Practitioners of each of these arts are also aware of the cultural and doctrinal influences on the individual and are capable of representing those influences as part of their recreation, or creation of human experience. In other words, while doctrines can attempt to interpret art, art also interprets doctrines and their effect on people's perceptions and feelings.

The most powerfully mimetic art is cinema, which reproduces many of the sensations of real experience. Hence, a film such as *Saving Private Ryan* in its opening sequence attempts to present, as closely as possible, a simulation of what the actual Normandy D-Day invasion was like—the sounds, the sights, the actions, the confusion. Of course, this is still only a simulation and the audience is not in any danger of suffering the pain the soldiers suffered in the real event. The medium does, however, put back much of the information that is 'missing' from, say, written historical accounts. Furthermore, the audience understands the conventions of the film and so, as in all the arts, they are able to 'read' the film to extract the meanings that the film-maker is trying to convey.

Poetry and prose do not resemble the feelings they convey but act to directly evoke certain emotions and thoughts in the mind of the audience. The creative writer or novelist seeks to convey experience within the limitations of symbolic language, sometimes using the very limitations of language to enhance meaning. The creative writer and the poet overcome those limitations by using words in non-standard ways. Poets have long recognised that words have meanings far beyond their dictionary definitions and that certain configurations of words can convey ideas and feelings that are far more complex and 'authentic' than those that can be presented by simple propositional statements. Writing, as an art, thus transcends the formal propositional structures of language to forge a richer, more experiential set of meanings.

This process has developed in parallel with the doctrinal use of language over the millennia and also runs contrary to it.

Perhaps most mysterious is the effect of music, which appears to be able to communicate without any reference to symbolic language at all. People with cognitive impairments who cannot understand written or even spoken language can be moved to tears or laughter by music, which seems to provide a direct link from the emotional centre of one brain to another.

Art can therefore be seen as an attempt to communicate the raw material of experience in an unmodified form, with the least loss of information. This is not to say that artistic communication is not coded but that it is presented in a code which conveys direct experience rather than a code based on a specific set of definitions. Unlike a purely symbolic code, the language of art does try to capture the 'look and feel' of what it represents. It is not only the shape of the body that is coded in marble but also some sense of its vigour and its erotic attraction; the painting of the mountain range not only codes the colours and shapes but also feelings of grandeur, mystery and sublimity; the moving two-dimensional image on the cinema screen not only codes the sights and sounds of war but also the sense of horror, tragedy and helplessness.

Hence, art seeks to create a direct connection that is less 'lossy' but also in some sense 'pure', that is to say, free from the interdiction of socially constructed interpretations. It may even challenge such socially constructed interpretations by exposing them to direct scrutiny, thus making us aware of the effects of such interdictions.

Of course, it would be foolish to think that art is not susceptible to doctrinal influences. Art is the subject of many theories and much social discourse, perhaps more so than any other field of activity. Twentieth-century art theory and criticism provided us with a great deal of impenetrable verbiage and it would be naive to think that art theory does not influence art practice. In fact, it is possible to surmise that much 20th century art employed many of the tenetic subterfuges of political and religious doctrines. For example, one of the advantages of non-figurative or 'abstract' art over representational art is that is it cannot be criticised on the basis of technique. Abstract art also rewrote the 'rules' for assessing painting and sculpture in the same way as many religions do. For example, when people in the early 20th century objected that modern paintings did not look like their subjects they were told that that was the point: the painting was not supposed to be a photographic likeness. Art was declared to be above representation in the same way that religion was above logic.

It then followed that because the layperson could no longer 'understand' works of art, the art world needed a class of art theorists—or a priesthood—to explain art to the public. All of these characteristics—subversion of basic criteria, shell construction, the creation of an esoteric language—place modern art well outside the proof zone, a classic doctrine with strong replicative tactics. We might also surmise that art has metamorphosed into this type of phenomenon because, like so many other doctrines in the 20th century, empirical selection mechanisms have disappeared. When people relied on painters to produce realistic portraits, because that was the only way their likeness could be preserved, inability to draw and paint was fatal for an artist. With the invention of the camera, that application of art almost disappeared and with it the selection criteria.[1] Now, technical skill was no longer a critical factor in the success of a painter or sculptor; what was critical was being picked up by the art establishment.

What this means is that art is now 'selected' by the prevailing ideas of the day. The dominant theories determine what kinds of artistic works reach public prominence.

---

1   A logical question might be, with the advent of the camera, why didn't painting disappear all together? The persistence of painting is a fascinating example of how a cultural practice can adapt to new circumstances in its environment.

Publishing houses, art galleries, theatre boards, magazine editors and film financiers have the power to decide which artists are funded, or exhibited, and which ones are marginalised. The artists regarded as the 'significant' artists in any period will be those selected by the intellectual elite of the day.

By contrast, art forms that have to 'work' for the wider public (that is they are subject to empirical selection) continue to work, as painting and sculpture used to, in representational modes. If non-figurative art were as important as art theorists make out, it is hard to understand why films and television shows for general audiences don't look like Picasso paintings.

Doctrines can also influence the work of artists by influencing the artists' perceptions and feelings. Artists, particularly artists who work in the world of ideas and words, cannot help but be influenced by prevailing theories of meaning and reality. Yet for all these incursions by the intellectual power structures of society, artists are still engaged primarily in the expression of experience and even when the experience they convey and the way in which they convey it is shaped (once more the popular word is 'informed') by prevailing doctrines, the works of art themselves still contain more information and are more communicative than any amount of theory written or spoken about them. To re-frame an old adage, a picture is worth more than a thousand words.

So, although artists, like empirical scientists, are as susceptible to doctrinal influences as anyone else, the work of both is still grounded in direct experience. Although we may think of art and experimental science as very different, they share a common methodology. They respond directly to perceptions, science concentrating on the external, art on the internal. Art and empirical science are the only reliable avenues we have of accessing truth through the phenomena of direct experience. They provide information that, while not unmodified by doctrines, is still the most unmodified-by-doctrines information we have.

EPILOGUE

FOR THOUSANDS OF YEARS human beings have thought
themselves the dominant species on the planet. With the
exception of gods and magical beings, people from the
ancient world until the present have seen themselves as
ruling all other species. In more recent times, Charles
Darwin postulated a process of evolution whereby species
were constantly succeeded by species that were better
adapted to their environment. This process, illustrated on
every evolutionary chart, seemed to culminate with the
emergence of homo sapiens as the most advanced and dominant creature on the planet. According to tenetics, however,
no sooner had humans evolved with their superior brain,
than that brain gave rise to a new species that would become
the real dominant form on the planet: the self-reproducing
thought system.

Now many people may object and say that a thought
system may be self-reproducing but it is not a species—not
a living thing. But suppose there was a microbe, a bacterium
that was capable of infecting human brains. Let us suppose
this bacterium, on gaining entry to the body, travelled to
the brain where it reorganised the neurons to cause certain

behaviours by the host that, although destructive to the humans, was beneficial to the bacterium—like a super version of the Sneeze Syndrome. Imagine it induced behaviours whereby infected humans would touch and infect others, while at the same time performing actions that eliminated competing bacteria. Imagine that human behaviour was totally subordinated to this particular bacterium and the entire structure of human society was designed to ensure its survival. Even though a bacterium is no more than a simple cell containing a set of chemical instructions, we would have no hesitation in declaring the bacterium as the dominant species and humans as no more than a host.[1]

By extrapolation, if we could acknowledge a bacterium as a superior species, then a set of abstract instructions that performs the same function, such as a doctrine, also must surely be recognised as a sort of life form, if not *the* dominant life form on the planet, for doctrines have utterly subjugated the human population around the world.

But what of consciousness? Can a self-replicating system be a living thing if it has no sensation, consciousness? This debate still pervades psychology and biology. While consciousness is a feature of life, particularly human life, it is does not appear to be universal since many life forms such as bacteria and plants seem to have no nervous system and demonstrate no evidence of sensation, yet are clearly life systems.

Here perhaps lies the central dilemma, possibly the tragedy of the human condition. Human beings, blessed with consciousness, are aware of their own motivations and actions and have the sense of deciding to do what they do. Foremost in the moment-to-moment operation of the human mind are the senses of perceiving, thinking and acting. The moments that most pain the human soul are those moments

---

1 . Many biologists and historians claim that bacteria are the dominant species
    on the planet as they colonise and exploit humans, and have also played a
    significant role in shaping human history to their own advantage.

when they find themselves unable to perceive, unable to think and unable to act. Their greatest triumphs conversely are those moments when they see clearly, act decisively and think deeply. How devastating to suggest, as the determinist and the teneticist do, that humans' whole perception of the world and the thoughts and actions that arise from it, are constructs implanted into the mind by an abstract program and that the perception of reality, which is so clear to the mind, is substantially an illusion constructed to ensure the survival not of the person, but the program itself.

This idea is as threatening to human sensibilities as Copernicus' theory that the earth was not the centre of the universe but simply a planet revolving around the sun. The uproar at Copernicus' suggestion in the terracentric world of the time was immense. It had been regarded as axiomatic for most of history that the sun, soon and stars revolved around the earth. Now, the world was, in one sweep, relegated from the centre of the universe to the third planet orbiting around a large ball of gas.

Since Copernicus the status of the earth, and humanity with it, has continued to diminish, the sun becoming just one of billions of stars in the Milky Way, the Milky Way becoming just one of billions of galaxies. And despite current attempts by some theoreticians to show that the 'probability' of intelligent life evolving is so low that we might be alone in the universe, the overwhelming conclusion is that humans are only one instance of billions of conscious and intelligent life forms in the universe.[2]

The suggestion that humans are not in control of their own minds but are manipulated by abstract information systems is as disturbing as the decentring of the earth, though as I have noted earlier, people have little trouble

---

2   Tenetics predicts that any intelligent organic system will be colonised by
      doctrines, leading to the hypothesis that if we ever contact intelligent
      beings from elsewhere in the cosmos, we might expect them to
      demonstrate similar behaviours to ourselves in regard to the promulgation
      and preservation of their belief systems.

seeing others as deluded, brainwashed and hypnotised. It is only themselves that they do not see as being so. At the same time, if we look at the history of philosophy and religion we find that humans have, throughout the ages, had a sense that ideas do have an embodiment outside their own minds and a sense of forces controlling their lives.

In the ancient world, the belief in gods evolved to explain external natural phenomena. However, gods soon came to be seen as affecting human emotions and behaviour. The effects of liquids in the body (the four humours), the conjunction of the sun, moon, planets and stars (astrology) and even numbers (numerology) have been believed at various times to control human personality and destiny. This suggests that people have always had some pervading sense of their lives being controlled by influences beyond their perception and control, and there was indeed a grain of truth in these intimations.

The idea that human beings are controlled by forces from another plane of existence is not so far wrong when you consider that doctrines, being abstract entities, in a sense are creatures from another dimension. They exist in a world that suffuses the material world but is essentially invisible and immaterial in the same way 'cyberspace' is both real and abstract at the same time.

Thus, the awareness of abstract forces controlling human affairs has always been there but the forces were personified and reified (as all natural forces used to be) as gods, spirits, vices, virtues, demons, genius, diseases, mental illness, or political and economic conspiracies. Tenetics simply relates these notions to something more recognisable, self-reproducing information systems that circulate through society just as computer viruses circulate through the Internet.

Yet tenetics does not abandon us entirely to the whims of these mechanical processes. Empirical selection promises that, if we can throw off the shackles of our prejudices and submit ourselves honestly to the universe, it will ultimately select ideas that work. At the same time, the fact of our own consciousness is irrefutable and our ongoing sensory experiences in their raw, uninterpreted form provide us with a continuous incontrovertible reality. Thus, we look to science and art and, even as doctrines continue to attempt to control our perceptions and our understanding, as artists and scientists we must struggle to be ever vigilant, ever rigorous and ever courageous in seeking to know our own minds.

BIBLIOGRAPHY

WORKS REFERRED TO IN THE TEXT

D.T. Campbell 1960 'Blind variation and selective retention in creative thought as in other knowledge processes', *Psychological Review*, 67(6), pp. 380–400.

N. Chomsky 1965 *Aspects of the Theory of Syntax*, MIT Press, Cambridge.

A.K. Dewdney 1984 'Core war', *Scientific American*, May.

M. Foucault 1985 *The History of Sexuality: Vol. 2, The Uses of Pleasure*, Random House, New York.

M. Heidegger 1975 [1954] *Problems of Phenomenology*, Indiana University Press, Bloomington, IL.

W. James 1991 *Pragmatism*, Promethus Books.

L. Wittgenstein 1953 [1912] *Philosophical Investigations*, trans. G.E.M. Anscombe, Blackwell, Oxford.

EVOLUTIONARY EPISTEMOLOGY

D.T. Campbell 1965 'Variation and selective retention in socio-cultural evolution' in H.R. Barringer, G.I. Blanksten & R.W. Mack (eds), *Social Change in Developing Areas: A Reinterpretation of Evolutionary Theory*, Schenkman, Cambridge, MA, pp. 19–49.

D.T. Campbell 1988 [1974] 'Evolutionary epistemology' in E.S. Overman (ed.), *Methodology and Epistemology for Social Sciences: Selected Papers*, University of Chicago Press, Chicago pp. 393–434.

G. Cziko & D.T. Campbell 1990 'Comprehensive evolutionary epistemology bibliography', *The Journal of Social and Biological Sciences*.

A wide selection of references to evolutionary epistemology can be found at *www.ed.uiuc.edu/facstaff/g-cziko/stb/refs_c.html#C*

RELIGION AND POLITICS

The Bible 1982, New King James version, Thomas Nelson, Nashville.

A. Hitler 1943 *Mein Kampf*, Houghton Mifflin Company, Boston.

M. Jordan 1995 *Myths of the World*, Kyle Cathie Ltd, London.

The Koran 1993, Penguin, London.

V.I. Lenin 1988 *What Is To Be Done?*, Penguin, London.

K. Marx & F. Engels 1939 *Basic Writings on Politics and Philosophy*, Anchor Books, Doubleday & Co, New York.

THE ORIGINS OF RELIGION

J. Campbell 1973 *The Hero With a Thousand Faces*, Princeton University Press, Princeton, NJ.

J.G. Frazer 1983 *The Golden Bough: A Study in Magic and Religion*, Macmillan, London.

R. Graves 1955 *The Greek Myths*, Penguin, London.

R. Graves 1981 *The White Goddess*, Farrar, Straus and Giroux, New York.

PHILOSOPHY AND THE DEVELOPMENT OF SCIENTIFIC THEORIES

D. Brian 1996 *Einstein: A Life*, John Wiley & Sons, Toronto.

A.C. Crombie 1952 *Augustine to Galileo*, Mercury Books, London.

C. Darwin 1958 *The Origin of Species*, Mentor, New York.

W. Dunham 1994 *The Mathematical Universe*, John Wiley & Sons, New York.

A. Koestler 1959 *The Sleepwalkers*, Penguin, Middlesex.

E.J. Lerner 1992 *The Big Bang Never Happened*, Simon & Schuster, London.

J.C. Polkinghorne 1984 *The Quantum World*, Penguin, Middlesex.

B. Russell 1961 *History of Western Philosophy*, George Allen & Unwin, London.

M. Wertheim 1997 *Pythagoras' Trousers* Fourth Estate, London.

SELF-REPRODUCING SYSTEMS AND MEME THEORY

S. Blackmore 1999 *The Meme Machine*, Oxford University Press, Oxford.

R. Brodie 1996 *Virus of the Mind*, Integral Press, Seattle.

R. Dawkins 1976 *The Selfish Gene*, Granada, London.

D. Hofstader 1980 *Godel, Escher, Bach: An Eternal Golden Braid*, Penguin, Middlesex.

D. Hofstader 1987 *Metamagical Themas: Questing for the Essence of Mind and Pattern*, Penguin, Middlesex.

A. Lynch 1996 *Thought Contagion*, Basic Books, New York.

H. Zinsser 1961 *Rats, Lice and History*, Atlantic Monthly Press, Boston.

POLITICS AND CULTURE

V. Bulgiosi 1996 *Helter Skelter: The True Story of the Manson Murders*, Bantom Books, New York.

W. Shirer 1967 *The Rise and Fall of the Third Reich*, Pan Books, London.

E.M. Tillyard 1963 *The Elizabethan World Picture*, Penguin, Middlesex.

INDEX